NATIONAL DE

Russian Social Media Influence

Understanding Russian Propaganda in Eastern Europe

Todd C. Helmus, Elizabeth Bodine-Baron, Andrew Radin,

Madeline Magnuson, Joshua Mendelsohn, William Marcellino,

Andriy Bega, Zev Winkelman

Prepared for the Office of the Secretary of Defense

For more information on this publication, visit www.rand.org/t/RR2237

Library of Congress Cataloging-in-Publication Data is available for this publication.
ISBN: 978-0-8330-9957-0

Published by the RAND Corporation, Santa Monica, Calif.
© Copyright 2018 RAND Corporation
RAND® is a registered trademark.

Cover image: Nikita Buida/Freepik

Support RAND
Make a tax-deductible charitable contribution at
www.rand.org/giving/contribute

www.rand.org

Preface

Russia is engaged in an active, worldwide propaganda campaign. As part of this campaign, Russia disseminates propaganda to Russian speakers in the Baltics, Ukraine, and other nearby states through a variety of means, including traditional and social media. In some cases, it has used this outreach to sow dissent against host and neighboring governments, as well as the North Atlantic Treaty Organization and the European Union.

The purpose of this project was to better understand the nature and effectiveness of pro-Russia outreach on social media and identify countermessaging opportunities. To gain this understanding, RAND Corporation researchers conducted a study that drew on multiple analytic research methods. These methods sought to accomplish the following objectives:

- Understand the nature of Russian propaganda on social media.
- Identify pro-Russia propagandists and anti-Russia activists on Twitter.
- Assess the degree to which Russian-speaking populations in a selection of former Soviet states have adopted pro-Russia propaganda themes in their Twitter language.
- Consider challenges confronting U.S. and European policymakers and offer recommendations for reducing Russian influence in the region.

In accordance with the appropriate statutes and U.S. Department of Defense regulations regarding human-subject protection, the researchers used human-subject protection protocols for this report and its underlying research. The views of the sources that these protocols rendered anonymous are solely their own and do not represent the official policy or position of the Department of Defense or the U.S. government.

This research was sponsored by the Office of the Secretary of Defense's Rapid Reaction Technology Office and conducted within the International Security and Defense Policy Center of the RAND National Defense Research Institute, a federally funded research and development center sponsored by the Office of the Secretary of Defense, the Joint Staff, the Unified Combatant Commands, the Navy, the Marine Corps, the defense agencies, and the defense Intelligence Community.

For more information on the RAND International Security and Defense Policy Center, see www.rand.org/nsrd/ndri/centers/isdp or contact the director (contact information is provided on the webpage).

Contents

Figures and Tables

Figures

Tables

Summary

The purpose of this study was to examine Russian-language content on social media and the broader propaganda threat posed to the region of former Soviet states that include Estonia, Latvia, Lithuania, Ukraine, and, to a lesser extent, Moldova and Belarus. In addition to employing a state-funded multilingual television (TV) network, operating various Kremlin-supporting news websites, and working through several constellations of Russia-backed "civil society" organizations, Russia employs a sophisticated social media campaign that includes news tweets, nonattributed comments on web pages, troll and bot social media accounts, and fake hashtag and Twitter campaigns. Nowhere is this threat more tangible than in Ukraine, which has been an active propaganda battleground since the 2014 Ukrainian revolution. Other countries in the region look at Russia's actions and annexation of Crimea and recognize the need to pay careful attention to Russia's propaganda campaign.

To conduct this study, RAND researchers employed a mixed-methods approach that used careful quantitative analysis of social media data to understand the scope of pro-Russia social media campaigns combined with interviews with regional experts and U.S. and North Atlantic Treaty Organization (NATO) security experts to understand the critical ingredients to countering this campaign.

We begin by gaining an understanding of the breadth and scope of Russia's social media campaign in the former Soviet states. *The near abroad* is a term that has historically referred to the former Soviet states, including Estonia, Latvia, Lithuania, Ukraine, Moldova, and Belarus.

The Kremlin aims to leverage shared elements of the post-Soviet experience in order to drive wedges between ethnic Russian or Russian-speaking populations who reside in these states and their host governments. Farther abroad, the Kremlin attempts to achieve policy paralysis by sowing confusion, stoking fears, and eroding trust in Western and democratic institutions. To conduct these campaigns, Russia experts argue, Russia employs a synchronized mix of media that varies from attributed TV and news website content to far-right blogs and websites (with unclear attribution), as well as nonattributed social media accounts in the form of bots and trolls. Our literature review paid special attention to the role of such nonattributed social media accounts, which are frequently but not solely employed on Twitter and Facebook. Indeed, Russia has established that, during critical moments, such as during the Ukrainian revolution, it can flood news websites with tens of thousands of comments each day.

We then searched for examples of pro-Russia propaganda within Russian-language social media content, specifically Twitter. To do this, we employed a recently established method, community lexical analysis. This method combines lexical and social network analysis in an iterative approach to identify and characterize different communities on Twitter, using data associated with accounts emanating from the former Soviet states of Estonia, Latvia, Lithuania, and Ukraine, as well as Moldova and Belarus. Drawing on community detection algorithms, we distilled 22,825,114 Russian-language tweets from 512,143 unique user accounts into ten of the most central communities.[1] Examining these communities with lexical analysis revealed two large and highly influential communities. One of these communities, which we call *pro-Russia activists*, consists of approximately 41,000 users who both

---

[1] In most cases, centrality is correlated with size, so many of these communities are quite large. However, we also include a few communities that are surprisingly central given their small size.

The data consisted of all tweets that met all the following conditions: (1) They were written between May and July 2016, (2) they contained primarily Russian language (according to GNIP's language classification algorithms), and (3) they belonged to authors in any of the six eastern European countries that had been part of the former Union of Soviet Socialist Republics—Estonia, Latvia, Lithuania, Belarus, Ukraine, and Moldova.

consume and disseminate anti-Ukraine, pro-Russia propaganda. An opposing community, which we call *pro-Ukraine activists*, consists of nearly 39,000 users who fight back with pro-Ukraine, anti-Russia content. Using lexical analysis, we examined the key themes and topics within each community. We also employed social network analysis to both understand communities' internal structures and identify potentially influential users.

We tested whether we could examine the influence of the pro-Russia activist community over time and in different regions in eastern Europe. To do this, we developed a lexical fingerprint of the content from the pro-Russia activist community. We then compared that fingerprint with that of eight longitudinal panels of Twitter users who were geo-inferenced to the region.[2] The goal was to identify the number of accounts in the Twitter panel whose tweet content statistically matched the pro-Russia activist fingerprint. The assumption underlying this quantitative approach, referred to as *resonance analysis*, is that Twitter users who use the same language content patterns as a known group of partisans share in that group's ideological beliefs. We show that 15 percent of users in Crimea and Donetsk share the same linguistic pattern as the pro-Russia activist Twitter community and that rates drop the farther one goes away from the zone of Russian influence.[3] After validating the ability of our method to accurately detect the pro-Russia activist community's lexical fingerprint, we argue that such a method could be used to track the spread of Russian propaganda over time in various regions, which could be a critical component to an effort to detect malign Russian information-shaping campaigns in real time.

---

[2] The data for the panels consisted of all tweets that met all of the following conditions: (1) They were written between August 2015 and May 2016, (2) they contained primarily Russian language (according to GNIP's language classification algorithm), (3) they belonged to one of the 2,200- to 2,600-person user samples in six specific areas in Ukraine (Crimea, Donetsk, Dnipro, Kharkov, Kiev, and Odessa) and two other areas in the region (Minsk, Belarus, and Riga, Latvia). These samples yielded between 500,000 and 900,000 tweets each.

[3] As we detail in Chapter Four, 15 percent is quite high because of the conservative nature of the resonance analysis method.

We also identified broader challenges affecting counterpropaganda efforts in the region. To do this, we interviewed more than 40 U.S. and regional experts on the Russian threat, current efforts to counter the threat, and recommendations for improving existing policy. Using these qualitative data, we found that U.S., European Union (EU), and NATO efforts to counter Russian influence in the region should consider several key factors. First, the relatively high presence of Russian-language populations in the region who descend from Soviet-era migrants and whose host countries have refused them citizenship gives Russia a unique opportunity to communicate with a sympathetic audience. Further, some government policies giving priority to national languages have limited government outreach via the Russian language, thus complicating state outreach to Russian linguists. Second, Russian broadcast media dominate in the region, particularly the Baltics. Ukraine is the exception, however: It has censored Russian government broadcasting and the popular Russian social media platform VKontakte (VK). Third, numerous social media activists, websites, news sources, and others appear to actively disseminate their own pro-Russia propaganda content without any obvious direct support from the Russian state. This makes identification of Russian-language bots, trolls, and other nonattributed content difficult. Fourth, the panoply of EU, U.S., and NATO actors engaged in counterpropaganda efforts challenges coordination and synchronization. Finally, we note that heavy-handed anti-Russia messaging could backfire in the region, given local skepticism of Western propaganda, as could the variety of dialects unique to the region.

Finally, we offer policy recommendations that are based in part on our analytic observations, as well as numerous in-depth interviews with local and international experts. Five key and overarching recommendations for improving the Western response to Russian information activities in the former Soviet space include the following:

- *Highlight and "block" Russian propaganda:* Identify mechanisms to block or otherwise tag Russian propaganda in ways that are both fast and specific to the audiences at risk. For example, we highlight the potential use of Google's Redirect Method, which uses videos and other content embedded in search results to educate populations who search for Russian-born fake news on Google and other search engines.[4]

- *Build the resilience of at-risk populations:* Introduce media literacy training in the education system to help Russian colinguists and others in the region better identify fake news and other propagandist content. Consider launching a public information campaign that can more immediately convey the concepts of media literacy to a mass audience.

- *Expand and improve local and original content:* To effectively compete with Russian propaganda, providers must offer alternative TV, social media, and other media content in the region that can effectively displace the pro-Russia media narrative. Among other recommendations is our suggestion to empower social media and other activists in the region by identifying key influencers and offering a series of programming geared to enhance their influence potential. We also recommend training of journalists and funding the creation of alternative media content.

- *Better tell the U.S., NATO, and EU story:* The United States, NATO, and EU should offer a compelling argument for populations to align with the West or with individual nation-states. NATO should further better communicate the purpose and intent of its Enhanced Forward Presence units now stationed in the Baltics.

- *Track Russian media and develop analytic methods:* Tracking Russian influence efforts is critical. The information requirements include identifying fake-news stories and their sources, understanding Russian narrative themes and content, and understanding the broader Russian strategy that underlies tactical propaganda messaging. In addition, the analytic approach identified in Chapter Four of this report, resonance analysis, provides at least one framework for tracking the impact and spread of Russian propaganda and influence.

---

[4] The term *fake news* refers to intentionally false stories that are likely seeded by trolls.

Acknowledgments

Many people contributed to the completion of this report. We are particularly grateful to many of the people who supported and participated in interviews and otherwise supported our travel to Stuttgart, Estonia, and Latvia. We also appreciate and acknowledge the assistance of Rand Waltzman, for offering his advice and guidance to this study. We are especially grateful to the reviewers of this study, Luke J. Matthews of the RAND Corporation and Sarah Oates of the University of Maryland. Finally, we are grateful to the Office of the Secretary of Defense's Rapid Reaction Technology Office for its generous support of this study.

Of course, any and all errors in this report are the sole responsibility of the authors.

Abbreviations

BBG	Broadcasting Board of Governors
COE	center of excellence
DNR	Donétskaya Naródnaya Respúblika, or Donetsk People's Republic
EFP	Enhanced Forward Presence
EU	European Union
EUCOM	U.S. European Command
ISIS	Islamic State of Iraq and Syria
LNR	Luganskaya Narodnaya Respublika, or Luhansk People's Republic
MFA	ministry of foreign affairs
n/a	not applicable
NATO	North Atlantic Treaty Organization
NGO	nongovernmental organization
RT	Russia Today
SNA	social network analysis
StratCom	strategic communication
TV	television

UA|TV	International Broadcasting Multimedia Platform of Ukraine
UK	United Kingdom
UN	United Nations
USSR	Union of Soviet Socialist Republics
VK	VKontakte

CHAPTER ONE

Introduction

Russia is engaged in an active, worldwide propaganda campaign. Information operations (or, in Russia's framing, information confrontation) is a major part of Russia's foreign policy, and social media are one important element of Russia's state-led information activities. A leading analyst on Russian information warfare, Timothy Thomas, writes that there is "a real cognitive war underway in the ether and media for the hearts and minds of its citizens at home and abroad" (Thomas, 2015, p. 12). A United Kingdom (UK) analyst of Russia, Keir Giles, notes that Russia "considers itself to be engaged in full-scale information warfare" (Giles, 2016).

In this confrontation, Russia uses propaganda, cyberoperations, and proxies to influence neighboring and Western countries. A state-funded Russian television (TV) network, Russia Today (RT), broadcasts abroad in English, Arabic, and Spanish. State-controlled news websites, such as Sputnik, disseminate news in about 30 languages. Russia also coordinates its covert information activities, such as cyberwarfare and nonattributed social media trolls or bots, with its more public media campaign, as was reported in the 2016 U.S. elections (see Office of the Director of National Intelligence, 2017).

Russia has made social media a critical part of this campaign. The Russian state's approach to social media appears to have become significantly more sophisticated following the antigovernment protests in 2011. The extent of the protests and their use of social media likely led the Russian government to significantly increase its efforts to control, monitor, and influence the internet and social media (see Freedom House, 2016, p. 8). Russia appears to also have invested in additional personnel to influence the domestic online social media debate, developing a "troll army" to complement bots, or automated social media accounts (Giles, 2016, p. 30). These capabilities were likely then adapted and expanded to be used abroad.

Russia has adopted increasingly sophisticated social media techniques, including sophisticated trolling on news sites, fake hashtag and Twitter campaigns, and the close coordination between social media operations and other media.[1] Russia's propaganda on social media appears to have multiple objectives, including inducing paralysis, strengthening groups that share Russia's objectives or point of view, and creating alternative media narratives that match Russia's objectives.[2]

Although Russia seems to have a near-worldwide scope to its propaganda campaign, one area that might be of particular interest is what it refers to as its near abroad. The near abroad encompasses numerous states, including central Asia (Kazakhstan, Kyrgyzstan, Tajikistan, Turkmenistan, and Uzbekistan) and Transcaucasia (Armenia, Azerbaijan, and Georgia). It also includes Belarus, Moldova, and Ukraine, and it has historically referred to the Baltic states of Estonia, Latvia, and Lithuania.[3] The Russian threat to these states is evidenced in Ukraine, where Russia has illegally annexed Crimea and has engaged in an ongoing hybrid warfare campaign that not only uses the famed little green men, Russian soldiers disguised as freedom fighters, but also includes a campaign of fake news, hostile Twitter bots, and encouraged protests. Other neighboring countries look at these actions and wonder where Russia will turn next.

---

[1]   Observations of the effectiveness of Russia's coordination draw in part from the example of Russia's reported attempt to influence the 2016 U.S. election.

[2]   Pomerantsev and Weiss, for example, argued that Russian propagandists see social media as an ideal path to spreading the idea "that 'truth' is a lost cause and that reality is essentially malleable." They also observed, "The Internet and social media are seen by Russian theorists as key game-changers in the weaponization of information" (Pomerantsev and Weiss, 2014, p. 6). See also Giles, 2016, p. 37.

[3]   Russian analysts and U.S. analysts of Russia are beginning to observe that Russia no longer thinks of the Baltics as within its direct field of influence, although it does retain elements of influence within the Baltics. See Radin and Reach, 2017.

Russia has several reasons for training its propaganda machine on the former communist countries. First, effectively influencing the political outcomes of these countries helps establish a cushion against what it considers malign Western influence. Second, some of these countries, including the Baltics and Ukraine, have minority populations of Russian speakers who are former Soviet citizens and their descendants. It is a matter of established Russian policy—specifically, what is called the *compatriot policy*—to protect the interests of this population and, more importantly, influence the population to support pro-Russia causes and effectively influence the politics of its neighbors.[4]

The purpose of this study was to examine the Russian social media and broader propaganda threat to the region of former Soviet states that include Estonia, Latvia, Lithuania, and Ukraine. The study also sought to identify potential strategies that can mitigate the Russian propaganda threat to this region. The ongoing conflict between Russia and Ukraine makes Ukraine an ideal location to consider Russia's propaganda campaign capabilities. We chose Estonia, Latvia, and Lithuania because these countries have significant Russian-speaking minorities who consume media mainly by Russian state–controlled entities. They are also European Union (EU) and North Atlantic Treaty Organization (NATO) members, which deepens the commitment of the United States and its allies to come to their defense and might make them more-attractive targets for Russia to undermine consensus within these bodies.

Approach

To conduct this study, we relied on a broad set of research approaches that include both qualitative and quantitative methods. Specific research methods are detailed in each chapter, but we provide a brief synopsis here.

---

[4] The compatriot policy applies to four categories: Russian citizens living abroad, people who used to hold Soviet citizenship, people who migrated from the Russian Soviet Federative Socialist Republic, and descendants of those in the three previous categories except those who identify with their new home countries.

Chapter Two examines Russian strategy and tactics for using social media and other propaganda methods in and beyond the Baltics and Ukraine. Drawing from published and unpublished reports, this chapter examines the aims and themes of Russia propaganda, identifies how Russia synchronizes its varied media outlets, examines the impact of this propaganda, and illuminates specific Russian social media propaganda operations.

Both Chapters Three and Four draw on recently developed RAND social media analytic capabilities to provide a deep dive into Russian propaganda efforts on Twitter. Chapter Three uses a method called community lexical analysis to identify a major battle of ideas that is currently being waged in Ukraine. We specifically identified communities of closely connected Twitter users in a Russian-language Twitter database geo-inferenced to Estonia, Latvia, Lithuania, Moldova, Belarus, and Ukraine. After surveying the content of these communities with a RAND-developed lexical analysis tool, we were able to identify a community of pro-Russia propagandists consisting of approximately 40,000 users, in addition to a similarly sized community of anti-Russia pro-Ukraine activists.

In Chapter Four, we employ a method called resonance analysis to assess the spread and potential impact of the pro-Russia propagandist community identified in Chapter Three. We do this by creating a linguistic "fingerprint" of the pro-Russia propagandist community and comparing it with the content from a longitudinal panel of regional Twitter users.

In Chapter Five, we identify the challenges associated with countering Russian propaganda in the region. We present findings from field trips conducted in January 2017 to Stuttgart, Germany, to meet with representatives of the U.S. European Command and to the capitals of Estonia and Latvia to interview government security representatives, U.S. embassy officials, and members of civil society. We complemented this with additional in-person and phone interviews conducted with U.S. interagency and NATO representatives and other regional experts.

Finally, in Chapter Six, we present recommendations for reducing Russian social media and other propaganda influence in the region.

We draw these recommendations from findings presented in Chapters Two through Five, as well as insights offered by our varied interview and document sources.

CHAPTER TWO

Russian Propaganda on Social Media

The literature review presented in this chapter provides context for Russian propaganda operations on social media, which are intertwined with Kremlin information operations via more-traditional media and other soft power elements.[1] In the former Soviet states, including Estonia, Latvia, Lithuania, Ukraine, Moldova, and Belarus, the Kremlin aims to leverage shared elements of the post-Soviet experience in order to drive wedges between ethnic Russian and Russian-speaking populations and their host governments. Farther abroad, the Kremlin attempts to achieve policy paralysis by sowing confusion, stoking fears, and eroding trust in Western and democratic institutions.

We also review a variety of more-technical analyses of how Russia conducts its social media–based information operations, including the use of trolls and bots (fake social media accounts that are fully or semi-automated or operated anonymously by humans). We conclude with literature that attempts to evaluate the impact of these operations.

Context and Aims of Russian Propaganda

Moscow blends attributed, affiliated, and nonattributed elements and exploits new realities of online and social media to conduct information warfare at a perhaps unprecedented scale and level of complex-

---

[1] Team members performed the literature review using keyword searches (including "Russian social media propaganda") on Google and Google Scholar and reviewing the most-relevant 40 articles.

ity. These information operations, which recall the Soviet-era "active measures," appear to be a growing priority within the Kremlin, which spent US$1.1 billion on mass media in 2014 and increased its spending on foreign-focused media in 2015, including to the widely consumed media outlet RT and the agency that heads Sputnik News, Rossiya Segodnya.[2] The Kremlin's social media campaigns cannot be entirely separated from its information operations involving traditional media, because traditional news stories are now crafted and disseminated online.

Moreover, the Kremlin's narrative spin extends far beyond its network of media outlets and social media trolls; it is echoed and reinforced through constellations of "civil society" organizations, political parties, churches, and other actors. Moscow leverages think tanks, human rights groups, election observers, Eurasianist integration groups, and orthodox groups. A collection of Russian civil society organizations, such as the Federal Agency for the Commonwealth of Independent States Affairs, Compatriots Living Abroad, and International Humanitarian Cooperation, together receive at least US$100 million per year, in addition to government-organized nongovernmental organizations (NGOs), at least 150 of which are funded by Russian presidential grants totaling US$70 million per year. In some parts of Moldova, local public channels charge for EU advertisements while airing, for free, the advertisements of the League of Russian Youth and Motherland—Eurasian Union, an organization whose Christian activism is infused with Russian politics (see Lough et al., 2014). In the Baltic states of Latvia, Lithuania, and Estonia, Russia's narrative is fortified in media through such outlets as the First Baltic Channel; in politics via political parties, such as the pro-Russia Latvian Harmony Centre; and, in civil society, by NGOs, such as Native Language, an organization that pushed for making Russian an official language in Latvia in 2012 (see Wilson, 2015; see also Auers, 2015).

Russian propaganda also blends and balances multiple aims within a set of information operations. Keir Giles at Chatham House

---

[2] On the Kremlin's spending on mass media, see Wilson, 2015. On its increase in spending on foreign-focused media, see Lough et al., 2014.

has pointed out more broadly that Russian propaganda aims to pollute the information environment in order to influence what information is available to policymakers or affects them via democratic pressures or to erode trust in institutions, such as host governments and traditional media, often by proliferating multiple false narratives (Giles, 2016). Andrew Wilson at the Aspen Institute divides Russia's outward-facing propaganda into three categories. The first is intended to induce paralysis through propaganda. The second seeks to target entities that already have entrenched worldviews with antisystemic leanings and nudge them in useful directions. The third attempts to fashion alternative realities in which a particular media narrative is reinforced by a supporting cast of pro-Kremlin political parties, NGOs, churches, and other organizations (Wilson, 2015).[3]

The Russian government's sphere of influence is global; it conducts these multifaceted propaganda campaigns in Russian, English, Arabic, French, Czech, Georgian, and a host of other languages. Pomerantsev and Weiss suggest that Moscow's influence can

> be thought of concentrically: in Ukraine it can create complete havoc; in the Baltic states it can destabilize; in Eastern Europe, co-opt power; in Western Europe, divide and rule; in the US, distract; in the Middle East and South America, fan flames. (Pomerantsev and Weiss, 2014)

However, Moscow's reach is most direct in the neighboring states and former Soviet republics that house sizable ethnic Russian and Russian-speaking populations, also called compatriots. The commonality of Russian language provides a springboard for common communication, as well as a potential issue wedge to leverage compatriots against their host countries and governments. In Chapter Five, we address the issues that cause the ethnic Russian populations to be receptive to Russian state messaging. This literature review focuses on the Baltic states of Estonia, Latvia, and Lithuania and the east Slavic states of Belarus, Ukraine, and Moldova.

---

[3]   The fourth category he mentions in his title is inward facing.

Russian-language Kremlin propaganda in these bordering countries draws on aspects of those countries' shared legacy as post-Soviet states. Themes include a common feeling that the West in the late 1990s betrayed them by failing to deliver on promises of prosperity; the supremacy complex of having lost superpower status; the idea that Eurasian civilization is founded on traditional conservative values, such as family and orthodoxy; and, finally, a shared fear of violent revolutions, in which protests are portrayed as slippery slopes to bloody civil wars (Borogan and Soldatov, 2016).

Drawing on these shared aspects, the Kremlin can leverage Russian-identifying populations to amplify the Kremlin's message, pressure those populations' host governments, and incite unrest in their host regions or countries. Furthermore, the mere existence of these compatriot populations can be used to legitimize Russia's status as a global leader whose protection is not only needed but welcomed outside of its borders (Zakem, Saunders, and Antoun, 2015).

In the "far abroad," Russian disinformation seeks to erode trust in institutions. Neil MacFarquhar argued that Russia paints a picture that European government officials are American puppets unable to confront terrorism and the immigration crises (MacFarquhar, 2016). Weisburd, Watts, and Berger divided Russia's aims with propaganda in the "far abroad" into four categories: political, financial, social, and conspiracy. First, they argued that Russian political content aims "to tarnish democratic leaders or undermine institutions" through "allegations of voter fraud, election rigging, and political corruption." Second, the Kremlin's financial messages erode "citizen and investor confidence in foreign markets," positing "the failure of capitalist economies" by "[s]toking fears over the national debt, attacking institutions such as the Federal Reserve," and attempting to "discredit Western financial experts and business leaders." Third, Russia targets social tensions by emphasizing and leveraging "police brutality, racial tensions, protests, anti-government standoffs, and alleged government misconduct" in order to "undermine the fabric of society." Finally, conspiracy theories stoke fears of "global calamity while questioning the expertise of anyone who might calm those fears," such as by promoting fears of the U.S. government instituting martial law or nuclear war between

Russia and the United States (Weisburd, Watts, and Berger, 2016). The common theme is the goal of creating confusion and undermining trust in Western democratic institutions.

Means of Employment

The Kremlin has built a complex production and dissemination apparatus that integrates actors at varying levels of attribution to enable large-scale and complex information operations.

Actors at the first and second levels of attribution produce or circulate exploitable content. The first level involves overtly attributed or "white" outlets, including official Russian government agencies, such as the Ministry of Foreign Affairs (MFA) and a constellation of Russian state-controlled, state-affiliated, and state-censored media and think tanks, such as RT, Sputnik News, the All-Russia State Television and Radio Broadcasting Company (VGTRK), Channel One, and the Russian Institute for Strategic Studies. The second level of content producers and circulators is composed of outlets with uncertain attribution, also called "gray." This category covers conspiracy websites, far-right or far-left websites, news aggregators, and data dump websites (Weisburd, Watts, and Berger, 2016).

Players at the level of covert attribution, referred to as "black" in the grayscale of deniability, produce content on user-generated media, such as YouTube, but also add fear-mongering commentary to and amplify content produced by others and supply exploitable content to data dump websites (see Figure 2.1). These activities are conducted by a network of trolls, bots, honeypots, and hackers. *Trolls*, *bots*, and *honeypots* all refer to fake social media accounts used for various purposes, but trolls and honeypot accounts are operated by humans, while bot accounts are automated. While both trolls and bots are typically used to push particular narratives, honeypots instead tend to be used to solicit information and compromise accounts via malicious links or sexual exchanges. Meanwhile, hackers deface websites, execute denial of service attacks, and extract secrets to feed content production (Weisburd, Watts, and Berger, 2016).

Figure 2.1
Russian "Active Measures" on Social Media

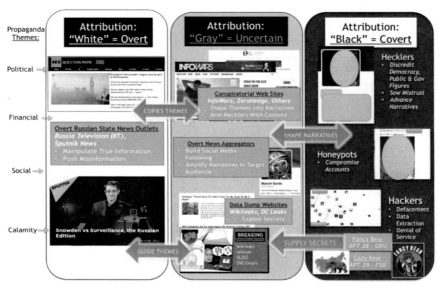

SOURCE: Weisburd, Watts, and Berger, 2016. Used with permission.
NOTE: A typical Russian disinformation operation, seeking to affect foreign
policymaker decisions via democratic pressures, erode trust in such institutions as
foreign governments and media, or achieve paralysis through the proliferation of
multiple contradictory narratives, is built in three parts. These three basic phases are
repeated and layered on top of each other to create a polyphony that overwhelms
individuals' ability and will to distinguish between fact and falsehood.
RAND *RR2237-2.1*

In the first step, false or misleading content is created by Russian-
affiliated media outlets, such as RT, Sputnik News, and Russia Insider;
Russia-friendly media outlets, such as True Pundit; user-generated
media sites, such as YouTube; and "leaks" from hackers, such as Fancy
Bear (also known as APT28) or Guccifer 2.0.[4] Second, force multipliers, such as trolls and bots, disseminate and amplify this content,
adding fear-mongering commentary. Third, mutually reinforcing digital entities pick up and perpetuate the narrative, whether they are ideo-

---

[4] On media outlets, see PropOrNot Team, 2016. On hacker leaks, see Weisburd, Watts,
and Berger, 2016.

logically friendly or simply fall under the category of "useful idiots." These entities include news aggregators, far-right or far-left sites, blogs, and users drawn in by clickbait headlines that reinforce their previously held beliefs, in addition to media outlets that frequently echo the Kremlin line but are not obviously affiliated with Russia, such as Zero Hedge (PropOrNot Team, 2016). Figure 2.2 shows the insular and circular nature of Zero Hedge's referrer network.

Figure 2.2
Zero Hedge Referrer Network

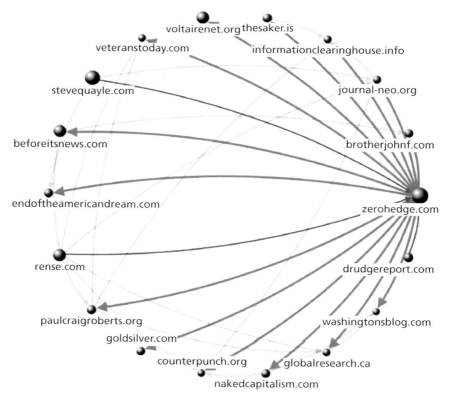

SOURCE: PropOrNot Team, 2016, p. 14.
RAND RR2237-2.2

Impact

The impact of Russia's disinformation operations in the near and far abroad is difficult to measure. However, there are some indications of the success of Russian media campaigns and other information operations. Some are anecdotal, such as Jessikka Aro, a journalist investigating harassment by Russian trolls for *European View*, who wrote, "Aggressive trolls have created a feeling of fear among some of my interviewees, causing them to stop making Russia related comments online" (Aro, 2016).

Other signs of Russian propaganda's impact are empirical. Gerber and Zavisca wrote in *Washington Quarterly* about a survey they conducted in Russia, Ukraine, Azerbaijan, and Kyrgyzstan in 2016. They found that,

> aside from those who never watch Russia-based broadcasts (who probably tend to be disengaged from politics), more frequent consumption of Russian television is associated with a greater tendency to accept the Russian narrative blaming the U.S. government for the Ukraine conflict. (Gerber and Zavisca, 2016)

There are a variety of reasons for the popularity of Russian TV among ethnic Russian populations; we explore these more in Chapter Five.

The impact of Russian propaganda in the near abroad is likely at least partially constrained by the extent to which compatriots identify with Russia or as Russians. Chatham House found in late 2014 that only "11% of Russian-speaking Ukrainians ally themselves with [the] Russian cultural tradition" (Lough et al., 2014). However, *The Guardian* reported in late 2015 that a Latvian government poll found that ethnic Russians in Latvia "are more supportive of Moscow's position over Ukraine than that of the west" (Luhn, 2015).

Russia's Social Media Operations in the Near Abroad

In the late 2000s, Russia began to explore its online propaganda capacities in the near abroad with a series of cyberattacks on Esto-

nian banks, government entities, and media outlets, supposedly conducted by Kremlin youth group "patriotic hackers" (Pomerantsev and
Weiss, 2014). With the invasion of Georgia in 2008, Russia disseminated multiple narratives online, providing alternative explanations for
its actions (Timberg, 2016).

However, observers point to the 2011 accusations that Russian
President Vladimir Putin's party rigged Russian elections as the true
precursor for the current incarnation of Putin's information warfare.
Putin reportedly blamed the West for instigating the protests within
Russia. In 2013, Putin declared during a visit to RT that he wanted to
"break the Anglo-Saxon monopoly on the global information streams"
(Timberg, 2016).

The annexation of Crimea in 2014 kicked off the debut of online
Russian propaganda on the world stage, which was followed by a diz-
zying swirl of disinformation about Russia's actions and intentions in
Crimea and Ukraine (Timberg, 2016). For instance, in July 2014, the
Kremlin advanced multiple mutually exclusive explanations for the
shooting down of Malaysia Airlines Flight 17 (Giles, 2016). One such
conspiracy theory was spread by RT, which "quoted a supposed air traffic controller named Carlos, who had written on his Twitter feed that
Ukrainian fighter jets had followed the Malaysian plane" (Pomerantsev
and Weiss, 2014). Fringe conspiracy website *Before It's News* posted
a supposed RAND Corporation document that had been "leaked,"
allegedly full of advice to the Ukrainian president to conduct ethnic
cleansing in eastern Ukraine. RT reposted the story. Even after being
removed from RT, it was cited in RT's opinion sections as characteristic of "guidelines for genocide, exported by the US" (Pomerantsev and
Weiss, 2014). The article is still posted on the website of Sputnik News
("Plan for Suppression of Eastern Ukraine Prepared by US Agency
RAND for Poroshenko," 2014). In August 2014, Maria Katasonova,
assistant to Russian legislator Evgeny Fedorov, faked her "on-scene"
news reporting with recorded explosion noises. In the video clip, she
can be seen starting to laugh, after which the lights are turned on in
the darkened room in which she had been filming (Smith, 2015).

This misleading content was amplified in Russia's near abroad,
even outside of Ukraine, using the force multipliers discussed, such as

trolls. Of the 200,000 comments posted on Latvia's primary online news portals between July 29 and August 5, 2014, one study found, only 1.45 percent came from trolls. However, for some stories, the majority of comments were by Russian trolls, as identified by grammar, content repetition, and internet protocol addresses (Boffey, 2016).

Given the wide presence of Russia in Ukrainian media space and popularity of Russian social networks, Russia was able to actively use social media to mobilize support, spread disinformation and hatred, and try to destabilize the situation in Ukraine. Hundreds of thematic groups have been created in social media and became a channel for distributing disinformation to, engaging, and influencing the public. In October 2014, an antigovernment protest took place in Kyiv, which included service members from the internal troops. Further investigation showed that protesters were mobilized through several VKontakte (VK) social media groups, moderated by Russian citizens ("Besporyadki pod Radoy gotovili grazhdane RF v sotsseti «VKontakte»," 2014). In the beginning of 2016, Ukrainian journalists exposed a network of dozens of social media groups, including Patriots of Ukraine, across multiple social media platforms, coordinated from Moscow. These groups used pro-Ukraine symbolic and nationalistic rhetoric to undermine trust in Ukrainian government and mobilize people for a "Third Maidan" (Samokhvalova, 2016). Social media are also used to spread fake rumors to undermine the morale of Ukrainian troops or discredit army leadership ("SBU porushyla kryminal'nu spravu za rozpovsyudzhennya motoroshnykh chutok pro Ukrayins'kykh viys'kovykh," 2015; "Shtab ATO," 2014). Other than social media, Ukrainian soldiers, as well as people living near the front lines, are sometimes targeted with directed Short Message Service messages, coming to their cell phones most likely from Russian electronic warfare systems (Digital Forensic Research Lab, 2017).

Russia's information campaigns appear simultaneously cutting edge and old school, potentially extending forward to the clever use of malware and backward in time to the publishing of books. In April 2015, information security company Trustwave reported that a Bedep Trojan malware kit had begun infecting machines and forcing them to browse certain sites, artificially inflating traffic to a set of pro-Russia videos, as measured by video views and ratings. This, in turn, made these videos more visible to users of the sites in question. Trustwave noted that, although the tactic of using bots to drive fake traffic is long established, "this is the first time we've observed the tactic used to promote video clips with a seemingly political agenda" (Kogan, 2015). That same year, multiple foreign-policy Western authors discovered that foreign-policy analysis books in their name had been published in Russian, without their knowledge, by Moscow publishing house Algoritm. Some trumpet that a "strong, united Russia is winning over its weak, divided and decadent adversaries" or support a narrative that Russia is besieged and persecuted by its enemies (Lucas, 2015).

In 2016, the Kremlin's information operations apparently continued to pursue simultaneous tracks of traditional and nontraditional media. For instance, in January 2016, automated complaints posted by bots on social media caused Twitter to block pro-Ukraine user accounts (Giles, 2016). At the end of that year, in December 2016, Russian news site Lenta.ru falsely reported that Ukraine had proposed taking in migrants from the Middle East "in exchange for visa-free travel into the EU," an invented story that was swiftly translated and picked up by a Czech news site, Nová republika ("Beware of NGOs," 2016).

This last example, of a Russian-language news story spreading to a Czech-language news site, serves as a reminder of the global scale of disinformation campaigns in an age in which borders provide no barrier to fake-news epidemics.

Russia's Social Media Operations in the Far Abroad

The Kremlin's information operations outside of Russia's near abroad in the past few years have ranged from disinformation spread by social media trolls and bots, to fake-news sites backed by spurious polls, to forged documents, to online harassment campaigns of investigative journalists and public figures that stand opposed to Russia.

One such harassment campaign kicked off in September 2014, after Finnish reporter Jessikka Aro posted an article asking for readers to respond to her with information about their experiences seeing and interacting with Kremlin trolls. Following publication of her article, Aro was dogged by fake-news sites and Facebook and Twitter trolls accusing her of assisting foreign security services and constructing an illegal database of Kremlin supporters. She started to receive threatening email, text, and phone messages (Aro, 2016).

Another signature harassment campaign appeared to blend with a larger attempt to leverage trolling networks, potentially in collaboration with Iran and Russia. In 2014, Weisburd, Watts, and Berger observed that, when Western foreign-policy experts condemned the regime of Syrian President Bashar Al-Assad, they would be attacked by "organized hordes of trolls" on social media. Examination of these accounts found that their network included what is referred to as "honeypot" Twitter or Facebook accounts: "dozens of accounts presenting themselves as attractive young women eager to talk politics with Americans, including some working in the national security sector," which were, in turn, "linked to other accounts used by the Syrian Electronic Army hacker operation." As Weisburd, Watts, and Berger argued, "All three elements were working together: the trolls to sow doubt, the honeypots to win trust, and the hackers (we believe) to exploit clicks on the dubious links sent out by the first two," while behind the Syrian network "lurked closely interconnected networks tied to Syria's allies, Iran and Russia" (Weisburd, Watts, and Berger, 2016).

Fake news advanced by Russian sources can easily be picked up and echoed by respected Western news outlets and influence search engine autosuggestions. For instance, in August 2014, Russian news agency Rossiya Segodnya commissioned a poll in France with poorly worded questions and a statistically insignificant subsample that RT used to back a story titled "15% of French people back ISIS [Islamic State of Iraq and Syria] militants, poll finds." The story and summary infographic circulated on the internet, initially appearing primarily on French sites. After a week, the generally respectable digital U.S. news outlet Vox ran the story, now titled "One in Six French People Say They Support ISIS." Although this effect has now worn off or been overwritten, for a time—despite a later story from *The Washington Post* debunking the claim—typing "ISIS France" into Google resulted in an autosuggestion of "ISIS France support" (Borthwick, 2015).

On September 11, 2014, a network of trolls and bots with links to Russia kicked off a series of operations targeting the United States with an intricate hoax referred to as the Columbian Chemicals plant explosion in Louisiana. In this campaign, thousands of Russian troll and bot accounts created the hashtag #ColumbianChemicals and forced it to trend, spreading news of the invented explosion in a sophisticated multiplatform (Twitter, Facebook, and Wikipedia) disinformation operation backed by digitally altered graphics and pictures. Most of the social media accounts used for #ColumbianChemicals had been in existence since the summer of 2013, claimed to be in the United States, and employed tweet-generating services, such as Bronislav, Rostislav, and Iviaslav, which are hosted by an entity with links to Russia's Internet Research Agency (Goldsberry, Goldsberry, and Sharma, 2015).

Accounts associated with this network of trolls followed up with a string of U.S. disinformation operations in 2015, advancing messages to exacerbate racial tensions, stoke fears of radical jihadi terrorism, promote pro-Russia stances, weigh in on U.S. presidential candidates, and undermine trust in U.S. government at state and national levels. In March 2015, these Twitter accounts pushed hashtags that included #TexasJihad, #BaltimoreVsRacism, #PhosphorusDisaster (which falsely alleged water contamination in Idaho), and #IndianaFedUp (which capitalized on antigay sentiments). In May 2015, these accounts ran anti–Hillary Clinton hashtags #HillaryFaildation and #MakeaMovieHillary, #SochiTalks (advancing a pro-Russia stance), and #ISISinGarland (to exacerbate fears about the Islamic State of Iraq and the Levant). In June 2015, the accounts executed campaigns, such as #TsarnaevsApology and #SurveillanceDay, agitating against the USA Patriot Act (Pub. L. 107-56, 2001). In August 2015, the network popularized #FergusonRemembers, #TrumpBecause, #BlackPickUpLines, and #NoGunsForCriminals and #GunViolenceOregon, the latter two pushing a racist and anti–Second Amendment message (Goldsberry, Goldsberry, and Sharma, 2015).

In 2016, as the Central Intelligence Agency, Federal Bureau of Investigation, and National Security Agency have assessed, Russia undertook an extensive operation to influence the U.S. presidential election, blending cyber- and information operations backed by social media activity (Office of the Director of National Intelligence, 2017). For instance, in October 2016, bots and social media accounts linked to Russia pushed a White House petition to "remove George Soros–owned voting machines," which do not exist, "from 16 states." The petition garnered 129,000 signatures (Weisburd, Watts, and Berger, 2016). In November 2016, as reported by *The Washington Post*, PropOrNot found that a single misleading story about Secretary of State Hillary Clinton's health that had been supported by Russia-affiliated outlets gained access to 90,000 Facebook accounts and accumulated 8 million reads. The *Washington Post* article also claimed that the Russian propaganda apparatus also spread a fake-news story (which had originated as satire) about an anti–Donald Trump protester being paid to demonstrate. Russian news outlet Sputnik used the #CrookedHillary hashtag (Timberg, 2016). That same month, PropOrNot claimed to have identified "over 200 distinct websites, YouTube channels, and Facebook groups which qualify as Russian propaganda outlets" that have "regular U.S. audiences," including "at least 15 million Americans" (PropOrNot Team, 2016).

In October 2017, news broke that Russia had exploited Facebook as part of its information campaign. Through the Internet Research Agency, Russia had created dozens of Facebook pages that sought to exploit and expand various social divisions within the United States that included race, religion, political affiliation, and class. These pages used Facebook advertising algorithms to target the ads to populations most vulnerable to the intended message. For example, Russia created a "Blacktivist" page that served as an extreme version of the Black Lives Matter movement. Advertisements created by this page issued denunciations of the criminal justice system and posted videos of police violence. In addition, the page "Being Patriotic" sought to rally Americans against expansions of refugee settlements. It also sent out missives attempting to dupe audiences into believing that federal employees were, in effect, seizing land from private property owners. And there was also "Secured Borders," which disseminated a video claiming that Michigan allowed Muslim immigrants to collect welfare checks for up to four wives each. Another site, "Texas Rebels," advocated for Texas' cessation from the union. Overall, these other pages reportedly generated 18 million interactions from Facebook users (McCarthy, 2017; Confessore and Wakabayashi, 2017). And new reports are now coming out that Russia also targeted YouTube, Google Search, Pokemon Go, and others.

Europe in 2016 also suffered a barrage of Russian propaganda operations. In the Czech Republic, articles proliferated on pro-Russia websites claiming that NATO intended to attack Russia from eastern Europe without approval from local governments. A poll in June showed that at least a quarter of Czechs believed some of these claims (MacFarquhar, 2016). Leading up to the UK referendum on exiting the EU (commonly called Brexit), Russia-affiliated media favored Brexit (MacFarquhar, 2016). In Sweden, forged documents and false and alarming claims about the supposed dangers of signing a deal with NATO were broadcast by outlets and amplified on social media in August (MacFarquhar, 2016). Daniel Boffey of *The Guardian* reported that Finland and Sweden were "being bullied by tales of Nordic child abuse rings targeting adopted Russian children" (Boffey, 2016). Also in August, a rash of tweets falsely claimed that Disneyland Paris had been evacuated because of a bomb threat; news outlets, such as RT, released stories citing the tweets, and Disney's stock dropped (Weisburd, Watts, and Berger, 2016). In Germany, the family of a 13-year-old Berlin schoolgirl of Russian origin identified as "Lisa" claimed that three men of Middle Eastern origin abducted and raped her. But even after German police debunked the allegations, Russian media continued to amplify the original story. In fact, Russian Foreign Minister Sergei Lavrov went on record, accusing Germany of "sweeping the case under the carpet" (Nimmo, 2017). In Turkey, Sputnik and RT falsely reported on thousands of armed police officers at Incirlik Air Base, and retweets claimed that nuclear weapons were being stored at Incirlik. Ten percent of the English-speaking tweeters of #Incirlik had the word "Trump" in their user biographies, likely representing some combination of manufactured accounts pretending to be Americans and genuine American Trump supporters (Weisburd, Watts, and Berger, 2016).

This suggests a cross-pollination between Russia's influence campaigns in Europe and the United States.

Trolls and Bots

The Kremlin's pioneering use of fake social media accounts that are fully or partially automated, as well as those operated by humans, deserves closer examination. Russian trolls and bots serve as force multipliers for Russian disinformation operations. For instance, during a period in the summer of 2014, the Kremlin troll army reportedly flooded *The Guardian*'s website with 40,000 comments a day ("Plan for Suppression of Eastern Ukraine Prepared by US Agency RAND for Poroshenko," 2014).

Life as a Kremlin-employed troll requires pumping out large volumes of posts through multiple accounts, creating the appearance of genuine engagement. Shawn Walker at *The Guardian* reported that, in Russia's St. Petersburg troll factory, employees are paid at least US$500 per month to manage multiple fake accounts, spreading propaganda and disinformation (Walker, 2015). Another source, Adrian Chen at *The New York Times*, cited a monthly troll salary equivalent to US$777 (Chen, 2015). On a given 12-hour shift, a troll generates hundreds of comments (Aro, 2016). Trolls sometimes operate in teams of three on a given forum: one to disparage the authorities and the other two to disagree, creating the appearance of genuine engagement and debate (Duncan, 2016).

A NATO Strategic Communications (StratCom) Centre of Excellence (COE) study of trolling behavior, systematically examining the comments sections of thousands of articles relating to the crises in Crimea and Ukraine, found that trolls used a three-step process of luring, taking the bait, and hauling in. In the first step, one troll would post a controversial, topical comment to capture readers' attention and provoke one of them to respond. The trolls would then wait for someone to oppose them, sometimes having to engage with the original post by clumsy opposition or exaggerated agreement to provoke the involvement of a nontroll. At this point, the trolls move to the third phase of the operation and "haul in," deviating from the content of the article and instead "commenting on selected statements to make the discussion antagonistic" and creating "the impression of a discussion, expressing 'differing' views on the Ukrainian–Russian conflict." The NATO study also characterized the following behaviors as indicative of a troll: copying "information not supported by sources" or pasting in links "without commenting on them," posting comments that are off-topic, engaging in conspiracy theories, intimidating or creating conflict internal to the comment thread, or assuming "the role of a false anti-hero," such as a "seemingly pro-Ukraine troll," and thereby "provoking responses from pro-Russian commenters" (Szwed, 2016).

Kremlin troll and bot accounts have evolved and diversified in order to expand their impact. The NATO StratCom COE has identified five types of trolls: "blame the US conspiracy trolls" to sow narratives of distrust, "bikini trolls" to engage with and draw out targets, "aggressive trolls" to harass people away from participation in the online conversation, "Wikipedia trolls" to edit blogs and other pages to advantage the Kremlin, and "attachment trolls" to repeatedly link to Russian news platform content (Boffey, 2016). Chatham House has observed that trolls also sometimes function as decoys, as a way of "keeping the infantry busy" that "aims to wear down the other side" (Lough et al., 2014). Another type of troll involves "false accounts posing as authoritative information sources on social media," such as @Vaalit and @EuroVaalit, two usernames that mean "elections" in Finnish. These two Twitter accounts appear to offer legitimate election information sources but actually spread Russian disinformation narratives (Giles, 2016).

This diversification of troll types also serves to help networks evade detection. Accounts with profile pictures displaying attractive young women, termed "bikini trolls" by Martins Daugulis from the NATO StratCom COE, can help Russian troll networks fly under the radar. Chatham House has observed that, because "these profiles attract followers and interaction from their targets," they can "defeat some of the tools for troll and bot analysis which were effective at highlighting and exposing more straightforward profiles" (Giles, 2016).

The scope of Kremlin bot operations is difficult to determine exactly, but many analysts and reporters have assessed it as extensive. For instance, in November 2016, a *Washington Post* article reported that Russia runs "thousands of botnets" (Timberg, 2016). Daniel Boffey of *The Guardian* reported in March 2016 that bot tweets and messages influence search engines in ways that benefit Russia, putting Kremlin-backed results into the top ten (Boffey, 2016).

In April 2015, internet researcher Lawrence Alexander conducted a study of pro-Kremlin bot activity and found 17,590 Twitter accounts, the majority of which exhibited characteristics highly suggestive of bots. In February 2015, Alexander had constructed a sample of friends and followers of accounts tweeting an exact 11-word phrase spreading an anti-Ukraine rumor about the shooting of Boris Nemtsov. Alexander thereby found 2,900 accounts that he identified as bots, based on suspicious network structure—accounts were highly connected with no outliers—and atypically low percentages of profiles with time zone information or Twitter favorites. In April 2015, Alexander gathered a larger sample based on usernames harvested from screenshots of alleged bot activity and phrases indicative of bot-like activity, such as tweeting the error message "RSS in offline mode," yielding a total of 17,590 Twitter accounts. Alexander confirmed that these accounts were largely bots, with less than 10 percent of the users having humanlike indicators on their profiles, such as location, time zone information, or Twitter favorites, and accounts almost never interacting with other Twitter users via replies or mentions, despite being highly active on Twitter, on average having produced 2,830 tweets. Many had Western-sounding account names (Alexander, 2015a).

These Kremlin bots likely boost the visibility of Russia-supported news outlets. Later in 2016, Alexander found that, on average, 20.3 percent of Russian-language news outlets' retweets were from accounts with bot-like behavior, higher than the 18.6 percent for English-language news outlets. The score for RT's Russian-language Twitter account was 42 percent. Almost half of the bot-like accounts that retweeted RT used one of several client software packages with names like "bronislav" and "slovoslav," which have links to Russia (Alexander, 2015b). In September 2016, an analysis by *The Economist* of 33,000 tweets from RT,

BBC, and *The New York Times* appeared to corroborate this finding. *The Economist*'s data team showed that the most-avid 20 percent of RT followers account for 75 percent of RT's retweets, a significantly more extreme distribution than for BBC or *The New York Times*. Furthermore, the team assessed that 16 of the 50 accounts most frequently retweeting RT are likely bots ("Daily Chart," 2016).

A study conducted by NATO StratCom attempted to assess the impact of Russian trolling and found at least some indicators of efficacy. The study team hand-coded 3,671 articles on the annexation of Crimea or the war in eastern Ukraine posted on a variety of Russian-, Lithuanian-, Latvian-, Estonian-, and Polish-language internet portals, as well as all of the comments on those articles. The study found that trolls' comments on an article tended be associated with an increase in the comments posted by nontroll users, possibly "just because they initiated certain discussion threads." The study also found that trolls' pasted links, however, were associated with a decrease in the number of comments. If an article used techniques of "denial . . . building/preserving the image of the enemy [and] fueling national, ethnic and religious hatred/quarrels," it was commented on more often (Szwed, 2016).

Summary and Implications

In summary, as this review demonstrates, Russia is engaged in an aggressive propaganda campaign aimed at multiple different national audiences to include its near-abroad neighbors on its western border. And of course, social media are by no means the sole platform of this campaign. Russia appears to actively synchronize social media products with those of various other information outlets, including Russian-branded TV broadcasts and web news, proxy civil society agencies, and web outlets. However, the Kremlin's web campaign that relies on anonymous web comments and nonattributed social media content disseminated by bots and trolls offers Russia the opportunity to target unsuspecting audiences with malign and often fake-news content.

Ukraine has seen the worst of this campaign, but, as watchers of the 2016 U.S. election know, the target set can swiftly change.

It will be critical for U.S., EU, and NATO policymakers to confront this information campaign. Key in this regard will be developing policies and operations that address the multifaceted components of Russia influence: More than just social media is at play. Investing resources in identifying, monitoring, and, if necessary, targeting the Russia-based nonattributed social media accounts will also be critical.

CHAPTER THREE

Pro- and Anti-Russia Propaganda Communities on Twitter

Communities form the backbone of the social media experience. Social media data are inherently relational; users comment on others' content by mentioning and retweeting other users, creating links and structure that can be understood using social network analysis (SNA). Assessing Russian propaganda's impact on social media requires understanding where in this network the propaganda exists, what user communities are sharing it, and which users have the most potential influence on the network.

In this chapter, we examine Twitter data to find evidence of Russian propaganda operations. We recognize that Twitter ranks only third or so in social media penetration in the region; however, we choose to use Twitter for several reasons.[1] First, Twitter is relatively easy to study because its data are public. Nearly all tweets, user profile data, tweets, retweets, mentions, and other "relational" data are accessible to researchers, enabling complex analytics on speaker, content, networks, and location. Moreover, as demonstrated in Chapter Two, we know that Russia actively uses Twitter as a platform, thus making it an ideal testing ground for our methods. Finally, although it is difficult to say whether our findings are generalizable to the region's broader population, we believe that the information learned from Twitter can serve

---

[1] In Ukraine, 38 percent use Facebook, 66 percent VK, 14 percent Twitter, 9 percent LinkedIn, and 32 percent Tumblr. In Estonia, 32 percent use Facebook, only 2 percent use Twitter, and 9 percent use Odnoklassniki. In Latvia, 60 percent use Facebook, 12.2 percent use Twitter, and 9.4 percent use Tumblr ("Internet Usage in Latvia," 2017; GemiusAudience, 2015).

as an important indicator. Local influencers detected via Twitter networks are likely local influencers in other online and off-line channels as well. In addition, the content and themes gleaned from Russia and Russia-supporting populations, as well as anti-Russia activists, likely swirl in other online and off-line mediums as well.

In previous studies, we have employed lexical and SNA to rapidly and correctly identify various communities and their key themes (Bodine-Baron et al., 2016). In particular, we examined the broader Arabic-language conversation surrounding the extremist group ISIS. Using these same methods, we were able to identify and consequently study distinct communities of ISIS supporters, supporters of the anti-Assad rebel fight, and Shia and Sunni nationalists. From the literature review summarized in Chapter Two, we assess that it is reasonable to assume that that Russian propaganda content, including nonattributed bot and troll accounts, would operate as a highly interconnected community, making community lexical analysis, as described in this chapter, an ideal method for finding and analyzing Russian propaganda on Twitter.

Approach

Our approach combines network and lexical analysis to relatively quickly understand the structure and content of conversations on Twitter using large data sets. We gathered the Twitter data using RAND's subscription to the full historical Twitter fire hose, through a contract with GNIP. GNIP, now part of Twitter, gathers social media data across multiple platforms and makes these data available for bulk historical and real-time purchase.

Because it was not clear a priori what search terms might reveal specific Russian propaganda, we instead gathered all tweets that met the following conditions: (1) were written between May and July 2016, (2) contain primarily Russian language (according to GNIP's language classification algorithms), and (3) belong to authors in any of six eastern European countries that were part of the former Union of Soviet Socialist Republics (USSR)—Estonia, Latvia, Lithuania, Belarus,

Ukraine, and Moldova.[2] The goal was to generate a comprehensive data set of what people in the former USSR in eastern Europe were saying on Twitter. In total, this yielded a data set containing 22,825,114 tweets from 512,143 unique user accounts.[3]

Following the methodology developed in similar projects, we first created a *mentions* network—a directed, weighted network in which each node represents a user and each edge the number of mentions between users.[4] Within this network, we searched for more–tightly clustered groups of users, using the Clauset–Newman–Moore community detection algorithm (Clauset, Newman, and Moore, 2004).[5] Then, to determine what made each community distinct in terms of the key themes and topics being discussed, we characterized a subset of the communities we found using lexical analysis. Finally, for those communities we determined to be most relevant to assessing Russian propaganda's impact in the region, we performed user-level SNA to identify influential users who appear to have large impact on the Twitter conversation. The remainder of this chapter discusses our analytical findings using this approach and highlights implications for combating Russian propaganda on Twitter. A full description of the methods used here can be found in Appendix A.

---

[2] To identify tweets from this region, we relied on the profile_geo enhancement provided by GNIP, which identifies users based on the information they provide in their public profiles. See GNIP, undated, for more details. Although it is not perfect, this approach allows for fairly accurate geo-inferencing of tweets and has been widely adopted for social media data analysis.

[3] Internet penetration rates in these countries vary from a low of 52 percent in Ukraine to a high of 91 percent in Estonia (Miniwatts Marketing Group, 2017).

[4] One similar project is reported in Bodine-Baron et al., 2016. In a Twitter mention, a user will include in the tweet content @*username*, the user whom the original poster wants to mention. This is also used in the standard format of retweets, attributing content to the original author. Thus, the mention network contains both general mentions and retweets.

[5] The specific implementation used was the cluster_fast_greedy function implemented as part of the igraph package in R.

Findings

Following the procedure outlined above, we generated a mention network containing 424,979 nodes and 2,871,849 weighted edges from our original data set of approximately 22.8 million tweets. Note that there are fewer edges than tweets; some edges include more than one mention, and many tweets do not include any mentions at all and thus are not included in the data set. We also excluded from the network any user who did not mention any others (an isolate). Figure 3.1 visualizes the core of this network (the users with the largest number of connections and heaviest edges).

Community Detection

Using the Clauset–Newman–Moore community detection algorithm, we found 7,773 distinct user communities. Each of these communities represents a group of Twitter user accounts that are more tightly connected to each other—meaning that they are mentioning each other more often—than they are to the others in the network. Several communities were large (more than 20,000 users), and many were very small (fewer than ten users). Because this number of communities is too large to analyze in depth, we used a standard "community-of-communities" procedure to reduce the number of communities to analyze, revealing two large *metacommunities*.[6] Figure 3.2 illustrates the procedure.

We then analyzed each of these two large metacommunities with RAND-Lex. RAND-Lex is a proprietary suite of analytic tools that RAND researchers created to perform rigorous and complex text analytics at scale. Specifically, RAND-Lex provides a test of "aboutness" through keyness testing for conspicuously overpresent or absent words. It identifies both individual keywords and collocates, or unique combinations of words that can then be analyzed in context by our language expert. Applying lexical analysis, we determined that the first meta-

---

[6] This procedure repeats the community detection algorithm on the network of communities (collapsing all users in a given community into a single node and all mentions between users in different communities into a single weighted edge).

Figure 3.1
Core Network of Mentions Among Russian-Speaking Eastern European Twitter Users

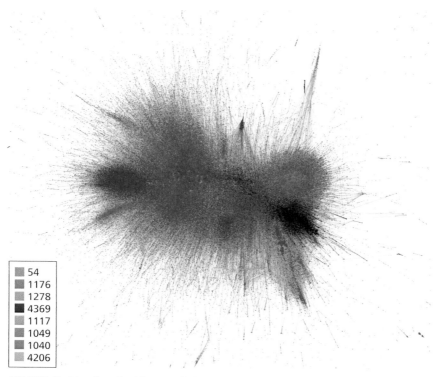

■	54
■	1176
■	1278
■	4369
■	1117
■	1049
■	1040
■	4206

SOURCE: Twitter data for May to July 2016.
NOTE: Each node in the network represents a single Twitter user. The colors represent the network community to which that user belongs, using the Clauset–Newman–Moore algorithm. The legend lists the eight largest communities, which are well-represented in the core network.
RAND RR2237-3.1

community (labeled *metacommunity 1* in Figure 3.2 and the related discussion) consists of general Russian-language speech and is not focused on any particular topic. The second community (labeled *metacommunity 2* in the figure and discussion), however, consists of more-focused and politicized discussion topics, including the Ukraine–Russia conflict. Table 3.1 highlights the keywords that are most statistically over-present in each community, as compared with a baseline corpus of

Figure 3.2
Community-of-Communities Network Analysis

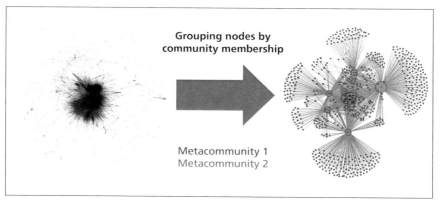

SOURCE: Twitter data for May to July 2016.
NOTE: The network on the left represents the entire user-level network, colored by metacommunity, while the network on the right represents the collapsed community-level network, also colored by metacommunity.
RAND *RR2237-3.2*

Russian-language Twitter. Informed by these findings, we focused our analysis on the more politically focused metacommunity 2.

Community Lexical Analysis

We selected ten of the most-central communities within meta-community 2 for further lexical analysis.[7] In most cases, centrality measures, such as in-degree, out-degree, betweenness, and eigenvector centrality, will be correlated with size. In our data, several of the most-central communities are also quite large. We also include a few communities for lexical analysis that are notably central given their small size. Table 3.2 summarizes their key characteristics and the lexical analysis

---

[7]   We measure a community's centrality by looking at a combination of in-degree, out-degree, betweenness, and eigenvector centrality of the communities within the community-level network, as shown in Figure 3.2. In the context of the community network, *in-degree* represents the number of unique communities with users who mention users in the given community. *Out-degree* represents the number of unique communities with users whom users in the given community mention. This is an unweighted, directed measure of degree (Hanneman and Riddle, 2005).

Table 3.1
Metacommunity Keywords

Metacommunity	Keyword	Translation
1	что	what
1	меня	me
1	это	this
1	방탄소년단	Bulletproof Boy Scouts
1	так	so
1	когда	when
1	как	how
1	мне	to me
1	lovebts	Lovebts
1	все	all
1	тебя	you
2	видео	video
2	новости	news
2	украина	Ukraine
2	понравилось	liked
2	россии	Russia
2	украины	Ukraine
2	россия	Russia
2	сша	USA
2	Помощью	assistance
2	Крым	Crimea

SOURCE: Twitter data for May to July 2016.
NOTE: "Bulletproof Boy Scouts" refers to a seven-member South Korean boy band formed by Big Hit Entertainment. Its name in Korean is Bangtan Sonyeondan, and it is also known as BTS, or the Bangtan Boys.

Table 3.2
Community Lexical Analysis

Community	Concentration of Geotagged Data	Users	Centrality	Lexical Result
1135	n/a	147	High, given size	Ukrainian business people
2435	n/a	212	High, given size	Ukrainian news
2613	Ukraine	1,108	High, given size	Network of bots
1220	Eastern Europe	7,480	High	Fans of Russian pop music
1127	Eastern Europe	8,056	High	Sports fans
1040	Belarus	17,207	Highest	Apolitical Belarusians
1049	Eastern Europe	29,776	Highest	Gadgets and life hacks
1117	Eastern Europe	33,864	Highest	Celebrities and show business
1278	Ukraine	38,783	Highest	Pro-Ukraine activists
4369	Eastern Europe	40,942	Highest	Pro-Russia activists

SOURCE: Twitter data for May to July 2016.
NOTE: n/a = not applicable.

findings. Note that the characterization of each community (shown in the "Lexical Result" column in Table 3.2) is the high-level summary that a Russian linguist assigned to each group after analyzing the lists of over- and underpresent keywords and collocates in the tweets belonging to that community, as compared with a Russian-language Twitter baseline corpus. Two communities in particular stand out based on this analysis: community 1278 and community 4369. They are similar in size: Community 1278 has 38,783 users, while community 4369 has 40,942, but they clearly differ in content. The conversation in community 1278 focuses on the Ukraine–Russia conflict and appears to promote nationalist pro-Ukraine viewpoints. Community 4369 also focuses on the same conflict but promotes a pro-Russia viewpoint.

In the next sections, we present the detailed lexical analysis findings and reasoning for these two communities; we include the others in the appendix.[8]

The Pro-Ukraine Activist Community

Informed by our lexical analysis, we determined that this community is concerned about the Ukraine–Russia conflict and is actively fighting Russian propaganda. We consequently assigned the community the label "pro-Ukraine activists." Overpresent retweets and mentions include Ukrainian news agencies and pro-Ukraine or anti-Russia accounts (such as @crimeaual, @krimrt, @fake_midrf, and @inforesist). Geographic names that are overpresent in this community are also related to the Ukraine–Russia conflict, such as Donbass, Crimea, Ukraine, and Russia. Overpresent keywords include several strong anti-Russia terms, such as *vata*, *krymnahsa*, and *rusnya*. The most frequent collocate (word pair) is "v Ukraine," or "in Ukraine," clearly indicating the community's focus on this conflict.

Discussion themes in this community include news and events around Russian aggression, Crimea, and eastern Ukraine, as well as Ukrainian politics, with a focus on anticorruption. Russia is discussed mostly in context of its intervention in Ukraine, war, and related sanctions. Also prominent are several initiatives aimed at identifying and exposing Russian propaganda—@stopfake, @inforesist, and @informnapalm.

Geographically, the users in this community are concentrated in Ukraine, much more concentrated than in the other communities we analyzed. Figure 3.3 displays the geotagged tweets from users in the

---

[8] RAND-Lex can use keywords to better understand the meaning of large text corpora. Specifically, lexical and lexicogrammatical analyses work poorly at the level of individuals' utterances because semantics and function at that level are highly context-variable. However, at the level of aggregates, these methods have high validity and reliability because word and word-type aggregates that vary in statistically meaningful ways show structural difference in text collections. This can seem counterintuitive because human readers experience only "serial reading"—one sentence at a time, doing human-level fine-grained context work, but never able to see large-scale statistical patterns. Decades of empirical work in corpus (that is, *aggregate*) linguistics support the notion that quantified lists of statistically variant words have meaning.

Figure 3.3
Pro-Ukraine Activist Community Geotagged Tweets

SOURCE: Twitter data for May to July 2016 overlaid in Google Maps.
RAND RR2237-3.3

community and supports our conclusion that this community consists of pro-Ukraine activists.

The Pro-Russia Activist Community

In sharp contrast to the pro-Ukraine activist community, this community clearly consists of consumers and disseminators of Russian propaganda. We consequently applied the label "pro-Russia activists." Retweets are mostly from pro-Russia media (e.g., @zvezdanews, @rt_russian) and Russian propaganda (e.g., @dnr_news, @harkovnews) accounts. Overpresent terms are specific to Russian propaganda, including #RussianWorld, #RussianSpring, #CrimeaIsOurs, and #Novorossia. One account in particular is mentioned more than any others—@history_rf—and is dedicated to highlighting Russian history. Frequent geographic names include *Russia, Crimea, Ukraine, USA, Europe, France, Belarus, Syria,* and *Turkey*.

The main discussion themes in this community include content from Russian media, such as Zevesda, Life News, RBC, and RIA. Top themes focus on events in Ukraine—Donetsk People's Republic (Donétskaya Naródnaya Respública, or DNR), war, sanctions, the Ukrainian military, and antiterrorist operations. Novorossiya, Donetsk, and Luhansk People's Republics are all discussed in a positive context, while Ukrainian President Petro Poroshenko, Ukraine, and the Ukrainian army are presented in a very negative light. Other popular topics include World War II, TV shows, sports, and dating; these are likely secondary content from TV channel accounts.

This community is more geographically dispersed than the pro-Ukraine activist community, as shown in Figure 3.4, with more geotagged tweets occurring in areas well within the areas of possible pro-Russia influence, including former Soviet republics.

Community Network Analysis

Viewing these communities from a network rather than lexical perspective reveals a very interesting structure, as shown in Figure 3.5. The two politically oriented communities, pro-Ukraine activists (community 1278) and pro-Russia activists (community 4369), appear to form two opposing poles in the community network.[9] Both have many small, exclusively connected communities, and multiple smaller communities are connected to both of them. The pro-Ukraine activist community has 135 exclusively connected communities, repre-

---

[9] Community 1117 represents a possible third pole in the community network because it has a very similar structure to 4369 and 1278, but, because it is focused on celebrity and show business topics, it is less relevant to the discussion.

Figure 3.4
Pro-Russia Activist Community Geotagged Tweets

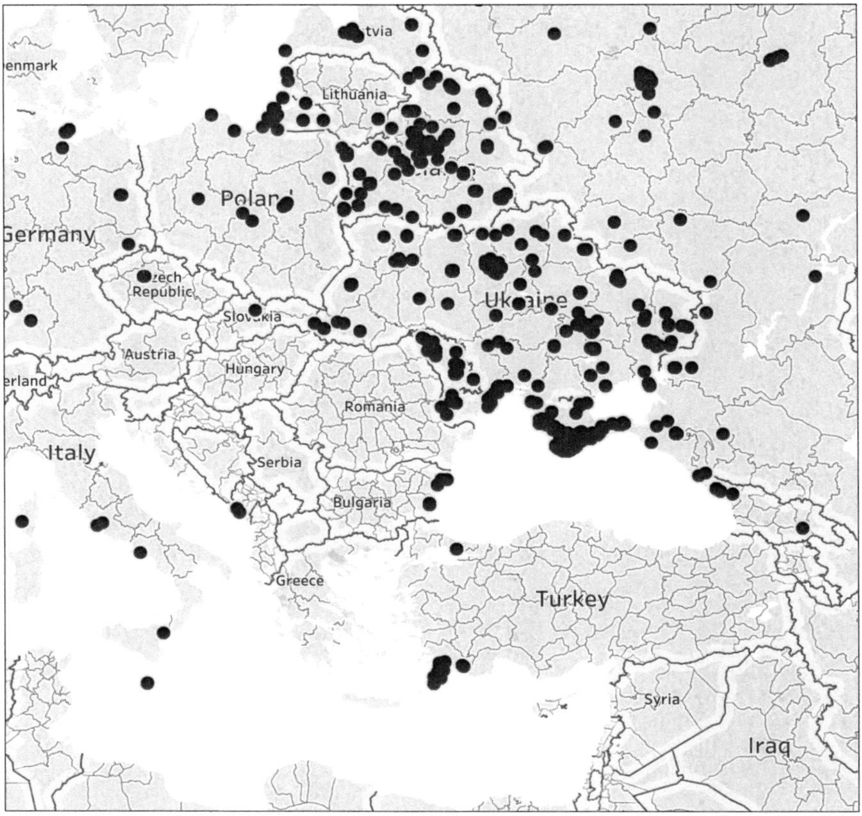

SOURCE: Twitter data for May to July 2016 overlaid in Google Maps.
RAND *RR2237-3.4*

senting potential additional pro-Ukraine accounts. The pro-Russia activist community has 51 exclusively connected communities, representing potential additional pro-Russia accounts. Those that are connected to both political communities (81 in total) could potentially be "fence-sitters"—accounts that are neither pro-Russia nor pro-Ukraine but rather could be swayed one way or another via propaganda and information operations. They could also represent a mix of viewpoints,

Figure 3.5
Political Community Network

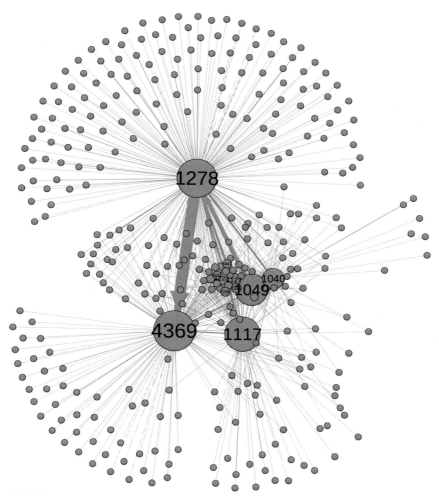

SOURCE: Twitter data for May to July 2016.
NOTE: Each node represents a community within metacommunity 2 identified using
the Clauset–Newman–Moore algorithm. The size of the node indicates the number
of accounts in each community, and the edge weight and arrow size indicate the
number and direction of mentions between accounts in each community.

RAND RR2237-3.5

pro-, anti-, and neutral. In Chapter Four, we will address this question using resonance analysis.

Although the two are similar in size, the pro-Russia and pro-Ukraine activist communities appear to differ slightly in strategy, as indicated by their network positions. Although they have very similar in-degree numbers (pro-Russia, 121; pro-Ukraine, 122), the pro-Ukraine activist community has more than double the out-degree numbers (pro-Russia, 75; pro-Ukraine, 168). This difference could indicate that the pro-Ukraine activist community pursues a more aggressive outreach campaign on Twitter, actively mentioning other accounts in distinct communities.

Examining the mentions between these two communities, we see that the pro-Ukraine activists, on average, mention the pro-Russia activists more often than they are mentioned in return, even when accounting for the difference in community size. Table 3.3 shows this difference. This disparity could represent the "identify and call out Russian propaganda" strategy pursued by many Ukrainian activists.

Alternatively, these differences could represent a more concentrated, possibly state-directed approach from the pro-Russia activist community. One particular aspect of state-directed messaging that has received a lot of attention lately is the use of bots for amplifying certain messages and themes. Although the science of bot detection is still being refined, some characteristics can be used to classify accounts as possible bots, including frequency of tweets, profile characteristics, and retweet behavior. We used Indiana University's Botometer program,

Table 3.3
Mentions Between Pro-Russia and Pro-Ukraine Activist Communities

Edge	Number of Mentions	Size of Source Community	Normalized Number of Mentions
From pro-Ukraine activists to pro-Russia activists	140,270	38,783	3.62
From pro-Russia activists to pro-Ukraine activists	88,936	40,942	2.17

SOURCE: Twitter data for May to July 2016.

to explore the prevalence of accounts with bot-like behavior, using a random sample of approximately 2,000 accounts from each community (Botometer, undated). Table 3.4 shows the results.

These results show that, at a statistically significant rate, more accounts exhibit bot-like behavior in the pro-Russia than in the pro-Ukraine activist community. However, the total numbers of accounts with this type of behavior are fairly small for both groups—under 10 percent—indicating that, at least with currently available techniques, it does not appear that bots form a large part of either community.[10]

Examining the user-level networks shown in Figures 3.6 and 3.7, we used network analysis at this level of granularity to find the top influencers in each community, characterized in Tables 3.5 and 3.6. Like we did to find the most-central communities but at the user rather than community level, we analyzed the network structure of both communities to identify the users with high centrality scores across four different measures: in-degree, out-degree, betweenness, and eigenvector centrality. A Russian linguist then searched for these selected users on Twitter and read through their 100 latest tweets, making a subjective characterization based on their content. Many of the accounts listed here are individual rather than institutional accounts. Pro-Russia activist influencers spew anti-Ukraine propaganda and frequently operate out of Russian or pro-Russia locations in Ukraine. Alterna-

Table 3.4
Botometer Results for Pro-Russia and Pro-Ukraine Activist Communities

Community	Accounts Classified as Nonbots	Accounts Classified as Uncertain	Accounts Classified as Bots	Percentage of Community Classified as Bots
Pro-Ukraine activists	1,901	466	133	5
Pro-Russia activists	1,506	492	169	8 ($p < 0.001$)

SOURCE: Botometer and Twitter data for May to July 2016.

---

[10] We note, however, that "trolls" or other state-directed accounts might be present in higher numbers; their behavior might or might not be bot-like.

Figure 3.6
The Pro-Russia Activist Community

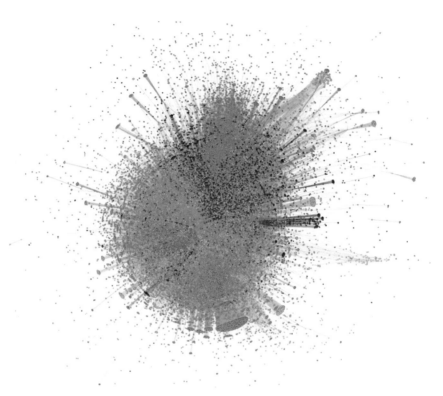

SOURCE: Twitter data for May to July 2016.
NOTE: Each node represents a user within community 4369. Node size indicates unweighted in-degree, and color represents the subcommunities found using the Clauset–Newman–Moore algorithm.
AND *RR2237-3.6*

tively, Ukraine activist influencers criticize, frequently using sarcasm, the Russian government. Analyses such as this can be used to identify key influencers in a range of Twitter-based networks and, as we suggest below, can play a key role in campaigns designed to empower anti-Russia influencers.

Figure 3.7
The Pro-Ukraine Activist Community

SOURCE: Twitter data for May to July 2016.
NOTE: Each node represents a user within community 1278. Node size indicates unweighted in-degree, and color represents the subcommunities found using the Clauset–Newman–Moore algorithm.
AND *RR2237-3.7*

Summary and Implications

From our analysis, we can conclude that many pro-Russia activists espousing a pro-Kremlin viewpoint hail from Russia and actively spread Russian propaganda on Twitter. However, state sponsorship of these accounts remains unclear and needs further analysis. However, one can envision Russia supporting these accounts either by creating nonattributed Twitter accounts that can serve as part of its bot and troll campaign or by supporting like-minded activists situated throughout the region adjacent to Russia. Further analysis could reveal the extent

Table 3.5
Top Influencers in the Pro-Russia Activist Community

Account Type	Location	Followers	Content
Personal	"USSR"	23,000	Hate posts about Ukraine and United States; praise of Russia, Josef Stalin, and Putin
Personal	Moscow	50,000	Hate posts about Ukraine and United States; Russian history
News	Donetsk, Ukraine	8,000	News about Ukraine; propaganda
Personal	Donetsk	18,000	Anti-Ukraine propaganda
UK journalist	UK, Europe, Russia	41,000	Pro-Russia
News	St. Petersburg	3,700	Anti-Ukraine "news" and propaganda

SOURCE: Twitter data for May to July 2016.

Table 3.6
Top Influencers in the Pro-Ukraine Activist Community

Account Type	Location	Followers	Content
Personal	London	2,000	Criticisms of Russian government
Personal	Crimea	38,000	Pro-Ukraine, anti-Russia
News	Kyiv	38,000	Affiliated with Radio Free Europe
Personal	Donetsk	19,000	Focus on eastern Ukraine conflict; shares names and movements of separatist fighters
Personal	Unknown	43,000	Sarcastic criticism of Russian government
Personal	Unknown	20,000	Sarcastic criticism of Russian government; coverage of eastern Ukraine

SOURCE: Twitter data for May to July 2016.

to which Russia is already supporting this group, either through bots or by providing particular content. Relevant U.S. government organizations could also use data from this group to identify specific areas and topics that are being targeted for Russian propaganda.

Activists in Ukraine appear to be central to the counterpropaganda fight in that they actively connect to fence-sitter communities, providing a potential option for expanding influence. Themes common to both the pro-Ukraine activist and fence-sitter communities would be "low-hanging fruit" to use for countermessaging Russian propaganda. Whether part of official U.S. Department of State messaging or through partnering with local organizations, this analysis can and should be extended to identify the key themes important to particular populations, allowing a fine-grained counterpropaganda message to reach the appropriate audience.

From a policy perspective, organizations interested in countering Russian propaganda on Twitter should consider identifying activists who are influential in their own and other communities and help to build their capacity. For example, @inforesist is an account associated with a counterpropaganda website, and @krymrealli is an account associated with a Ukrainian news site—both are highly influential in the pro-Ukraine activist community. Gathering the relevant Twitter data is relatively inexpensive and easy, and the network analysis required to identify key influencers is not particularly computationally expensive. The results could then be used to reach out to identified users and offer support, through either training or resources.

On the other side of the debate, network analysis can also be used to identify central users in the pro-Russia activist community. It is possible that some of these are bots or trolls and could be flagged for suspension for violating Twitter's terms of service. Further analysis could be performed to confirm whether Twitter is actively removing such accounts, and, if not, relevant U.S. and other government organizations could use such findings to encourage Twitter to expand and improve their bot detection and removal algorithms. Alternatively, identifying accounts as sources of propaganda—"calling them out"—might be helpful to prevent the spread of their message to audiences that otherwise would consider them factual.

CHAPTER FOUR

Resonance Analysis of Pro-Russia Activists

Given the potential that Russian propaganda on social media has to affect events around the world, it is vitally important to understand its extent and impact. In this chapter, we propose and test a method that can be used to assess the effect that Russian propaganda has on Twitter. We specifically assess the prevalence of those disseminating pro-Russia, anti-Ukraine content akin to that of the pro-Russia activist community described in Chapter Three.

Although our analysis focuses exclusively on Twitter, which admittedly is not the dominant platform in all areas of the world, it serves well as a testing ground for developing approaches to quantify this impact. *Resonance analysis* is a developing methodology for identifying statistical differences in how social groups use language and quantifying how common those statistical differences are within a larger population. In essence, it hypothesizes how much affinity might exist for a specific group within a general population, based on the language its members employ.

Theoretical Foundation

Language is a versatile tool kit for expressing ideas. Its versatility is demonstrated not only in the ideological complexity it can convey but also in the variety of ways that the same idea can be formulated as language. Because language is so versatile, there is ample room for individual people and groups of people to use it in distinctive ways. Consequently, there are many variations within any language, and they correspond to meaningful distinctions in social organization—geographic variation, subcultures, formal organizations, and advocacy groups (*publics*), among others.[1] These differences perpetuate themselves through intention, habit, and unconscious reaction. Resonance analysis exploits the close connection between social structure and language. It identifies how language use within a particular *group of interest* is distinct from language use in a general *baseline population*, and then searches for that distinctive *language signature* within a *target population*.[2] Through this process, resonance analysis hypothesizes how much linguistic—and thereby social—affinity exists between a *target population* and a *group of interest*.

Approach

Resonance analysis is about measuring how much any given populace uses the distinctive language of a group of interest. In essence, we derive a signature of what is distinctive about a group's language use, then measure the social media talk, user by user in a region, for how close the match is. If user A has little or no match with the signature, user A and the group are not resonant; if user B exceeds match thresholds, user B and the group are resonant. In this chapter, we develop resonance analysis toward the challenge of detecting Twitter users in select areas of former-USSR eastern Europe who use language in a manner reminiscent of the community of users identified in Chapter Three as pro-Russia activists. This might be useful specifically for understanding pro-Russia influence operations in the region and, more generally, in developing a computationally inexpensive approach for mapping affinities for a group of interest within a larger social media population.

---

[1] A public is "that portion of the populace engaged in evolving shared opinion on a particular issue, with the intent of influencing its resolution. They are not fixed and they are not idealized constructs, they are *emergences*" (Hauser, 2002, p. 85 [emphasis in the original]). See also Kaufer and Butler, 2010.

[2] The distinctive words in the source text, as compared with the baseline text, make up a list of keywords. Together with the keywords' keyness scores, the list is referred to as a *signature*.

We discovered through this analysis that distinguishing between two sides of a debate requires a more specific set of signatures and baseline text than previously thought. Because opposing groups tend to discuss the same topics, the baseline text must be pertinent to that particular discussion, and two signatures are required to distinguish between them, in addition to a "topic" signature to identify the debate itself, as outlined here and in Figure 4.1:

- *pro-Russia activist signature corpus:* 1,882,520 tweets from 9,989 users within the pro-Russia activist community. Note that these are tweets from a subset of the total users in that community.

- *pro-Ukraine activist signature corpus:* 4,158,122 tweets from 9,823 accounts in the pro-Ukraine activist community. Note that these are tweets from a subset of the total users in that community.

- *partisan baseline corpus:* pro-Russia activist signature corpus combined with pro-Ukraine activist signature corpus (6,040,642 tweets from 19,812 accounts)

- *topic signature corpus:* pro-Russia activist signature corpus combined with pro-Ukraine activist signature corpus (6,040,642 tweets from 19,812 accounts). Note that this is the same as the partisan baseline corpus.

- *topic baseline corpus:* 21,382,230 Russian-language (according to GNIP's language classification algorithms) tweets from 226,141 users across Estonia, Latvia, Lithuania, Belarus, Ukraine, and Moldova[3]

- *target population corpus:* all tweets that meet all these conditions:
  - were written between August 2015 and May 2016
  - contain primarily Russian language
  - belong to one of the 2,200- to 2,600-person user samples in six specific areas in Ukraine (Crimea, Donetsk, Dnipro, Kharkov, Kyiv, and Odessa) and two other areas in the region (Minsk,

---

[3] Note that this is a subset of the total data used in the lexical and network analyses described in Chapter Three. We screened accounts for verbosity.

Figure 4.1
The Corpora in Our Analysis

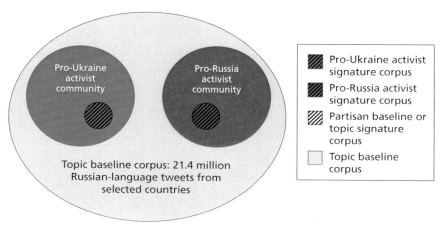

Belarus, and Riga, Latvia). These samples yielded between 500,000 and 900,000 tweets each.

For best results, we have found that all corpora should be drawn from text that is written in the same language (in this case, Russian), is generated in the same medium (in this case, tweets), and contains enough users to cancel out the language-use idiosyncrasies of any particular user. Ideally, corpora would also be drawn over a sufficiently long period of time to cancel out trends in word use due to any particular current event. Otherwise, the signature will become increasingly ineffective as that event recedes into the past.

For each corpus, we then regularized the text by removing punctuation, regularizing spacing and capitalization, and performing other such processing to enhance the signal-to-noise ratio. For additional details on this process, see Appendix A. Once the text was regularized, we formulated the signatures by performing keyness testing with log likelihood scoring to find the distinctive words in the signature text as compared with the baseline text (Baker et al., 2008, p. 273; Scott, 2008, p. 110). Specifically, we did the following:

1. Count the numbers of times that words and two-word collocates appear in the signature and baseline text.
2. Calculate keyness scores for every word and collocate in the signature corpus that also appears in the baseline corpus:

$$L = 2\left(\begin{array}{l} f_p \times \log \dfrac{f_p}{N_p \times \left(f_p + f_r\right) \times N_t^{-1}} \\[2em] + f_r \times \log \dfrac{f_r}{N_r \times \left(f_p + f_r\right) \times N_t^{-1}} \end{array}\right),$$

where

f_p = the number of times the word appeared
  in a specific reference corpus

f_r = the number of times the word appears
  in the general corpus

N_p = the total number of words examined
  in a specific reference corpus

N_r = the total number of words examined
  in the general corpus

N_t = the total number of words examined
  in both reference and general corpora.

3. Truncate score outliers so that no small subset of words can drive resonance scores on its own. The truncation threshold is currently 100 times the median word keyness score. The 100-time median threshold is not immutable. Any reasonable outlier truncation strategy will suffice, as long as it keeps outlier keywords from dominating the resulting scores.
4. Discard collocates if the collocate keyness score is not equal to or greater than 1 percent of the sum of keyness scores for its component terms. For example, if the word "two" and the word "words" each had a keyness score of 100, the phrase "two words"

would need a keyness score of at least 2 to not be discarded from the signature. If computational resources are sufficient, there is no harm in keeping in all collocates. However, they are unlikely to have a significant impact on the final resonance scores if they do not meet this criterion.

This process could yield thousands of words that score as (at least mildly) distinctive of one group compared with the baseline. We generally used all of them as the signature because the highest-quality resonance scores are the ones in which no small subset of terms dominates the outcome.

We then calculated the average keyword score per word for each user in the signature, baseline, and test texts. To do this, we summed a keyness score for each word used in a tweet from each user and divided by the total number of words:

$$\frac{\Sigma\left(S_G \times N_U\right)}{\Sigma N_U},$$

where

S_G = the signature vector for a group of interest

(outliers truncated to 100 times the median)

N_U = the vector of the number of times the user wrote each word

(cumulative for all tweets).

This step is particularly important for population assessment because it keeps high-volume tweeters from drowning out low-volume tweeters.

The last step in the resonance analysis process is to identify resonant users. For many applications, this involves using the baseline text to determine what level of resonance score could likely occur by chance alone, and then setting a threshold higher than what one would expect at random. However, we have found that partisans on opposing sides of a conflict (such as our pro-Russia activist and pro-Ukraine activist communities) talk more like each other than like the general public.

Consequently, they both score highly on signatures developed against a general population baseline. To compensate for this similarity, we employed a two-stage resonance process. The first stage calculates a signature (the topic signature) that distinguishes partisans of either side from the baseline general population. The second stage uses a signature ratio procedure (the partisan signature) to distinguish partisans of one side (i.e., pro-Russia activists) from partisans of the other side, using only topic-resonant content as a baseline. We labeled a user as resonant with the pro-Russia activist community if the user scored as resonant with both the first-stage topic signature *and* the second-stage partisanship signature. The procedure is as follows and is described in more detail in Appendix A:

1. Identify a moderately large number of users (set P) who are known partisans of each group. In this case, we used the members of the pro-Russia and pro-Ukraine activist communities.
2. Calculate the resonance score for all users in P using the topic signature.
3. Choose a threshold such that most accounts in P are topic resonant. For this analysis, we converted topic scores into z-score units for ease of analysis, and then chose $\sigma = 0.5$ as our threshold.
4. Calculate the resonance score for all users in P using the partisan signatures (in this case, the pro-Russia activist signature and the pro-Ukraine activist signature). Express each score as a ratio, and truncate the ratios at ±2. Choose a threshold such that true positives for users in P are maximized while false positives remain below 5 percent. The 0.6 threshold achieves a 73-percent true positive and 4-percent false positive rate.[4]
5. Finally, calculate the topic- and partisan-resonance scores for all users in the test population.

---

[4] Note that these are very conservative ratios. We chose them so that we would have high confidence in any matches, at the cost of likely not identifying all the resonant users in the population.

6. Applying the determined thresholds, identify users who are resonant with both the topic and partisan signatures.

Method Validation
Signature Scoring of Known Partisans
To validate the approach outlined in the preceding section, we first tested how well our method worked to categorize the users we used for the signature derivation. Specifically, we scored the members of the pro-Ukraine activist and pro-Russia activist communities against the topic and partisan signatures. This is essentially a common-sense check to ensure that our signatures represent what we believe them to represent.

If our procedure executes accurately, it should label members of both communities as resonant with the topic signature and just the pro-Russia activist community as resonant with the pro-Russia activist signature. Table 4.1 reports the percentage of users in each community labeled resonant with each signature. Although the detection rate is not perfect, the majority of accounts are labeled resonant with the signatures with which we would expect them to be resonant. This suggests that the methodology can distinguish between partisans, even when they are vigorously discussing the same subjects.

Comparison of Human and Resonance Analysis User Labeling
Because the previous validation was a basic self-check, we also validated the method against a human analyst's ability to distinguish between pro- and anti-Russia content, with a single-blind, out-of-sample test of the methodology. We randomly sampled 60 users from our longi-

Table 4.1
Known-Partisan Validity Test, as Percentages of Communities

Community	Topic Signature	Pro-Russia Activist Signature
Pro-Ukraine activists	65	11
Pro-Russia activists	59	74

NOTE: This table shows the percentage of users in each community who exceeded the resonance thresholds for the topic and pro-Russia activist signatures, respectively.

tudinal panel data, each of whom had tweeted at least 1,000 words total and had tweeted at least once in at least five of the nine months in that data sample.[5] Of the 60, 15 each met exclusively one of these four criteria:

- *not resonant:* These users scored neither as topic resonant nor as pro-Russia activist resonant. This means that, compared with the baseline population, they did not favor the topics of interest to the pro- or anti-Russia partisans. It also means that, compared with users who favored those topics, they were not more likely to use language that the pro-Russia activist community members favored.
- *topic resonant:* These users were topic resonant but not partisan resonant. That is, they favored the topics that were more of interest to our pro- and anti-Russia partisans than to the general public but did not favor language that members of the pro-Russia activist community employed.
- *partisan resonant:* These users were not topic resonant but were partisan resonant. That is, they tended to make word choices that were more commonly found among pro-Russia partisans than among anti-Russia partisans, but only once we factored out differences in topic preference.
- *likely Russian propaganda supporter:* These users were resonant with both the topic and pro-Russia activist signatures. That is, they met both criteria necessary to label them as using language characteristic of consumers and disseminators of Russian propaganda.

An expert on Russian language examined these accounts on Twitter (without being told which accounts were in which category)

---

[5] This means not only that there was sufficient content for each user but also that that content was not limited to a single short time period.

and rated each account on a five-point Likert scale, according to these two criteria:

- This account favors about the same topics that are of special interest to pro-Russia activist and pro-Ukraine activist accounts (i.e., favors the same topics as community 4369 *and* community 1278)
    - ☐ strongly agree (5)
    - ☐ agree (4)
    - ☐ insufficient or ambiguous data (3)
    - ☐ disagree (2)
    - ☐ strongly disagree (1)
- This account is pro-Russia propaganda (i.e., worldview seems similar to those of accounts in community 1278)
    - ☐ strongly agree (5)
    - ☐ agree (4)
    - ☐ insufficient or ambiguous data (3)
    - ☐ disagree (2)
    - ☐ strongly disagree (1).

Table 4.2 reveals the mean rating for accounts in each group. On average, the Russian-language expert rated likely Russian propaganda supporter accounts as pro-Russia propaganda and all other groups as not pro-Russia propaganda. This difference in means is highly statistically significant. The expert also rated both likely supporters of Russian propaganda and topic-resonant accounts as discussing partisan-favored topics. The difference in means for this rating was also statistically significant.

Phrased in the language of detection, resonance analysis correctly identified 71 percent of the pro-Russia activist accounts as likely supporters of Russian propaganda (the "positive prediction" accuracy) and 90 percent of the other accounts as not likely supporters of Russian propaganda (the "negative prediction" accuracy).[6] This totals to an 83-percent true positive rate, at the cost of only an 8-percent false positive rate. In summary, the expert scoring was highly consistent with the

---

[6] We used >3.5 (agree or strongly agree) as a cutoff point.

Table 4.2
Analyst's Mean Rating of Computer-Labeled Accounts (Single-Blind Test)

Group	Discusses Favored Topics	Appears to Disseminate and Consume Pro-Russia Propaganda
Likely supporter of Russian propaganda	3.9***	4.0***
Topic resonant	4.0***	1.6
Partisan resonant	1.3	1.2
Not resonant	1.6	1.2

NOTE: *** = statistical significance at the $p < 0.001$ level. For the "Discusses Favored Topics" column, we conducted t-tests assessing the difference in mean rating of likely supporter of Russian propaganda and topic-resonant accounts versus partisan-resonant and not-resonant accounts. For "Appears to Disseminate and Consume Pro-Russia Propaganda," we compared the difference in mean rating of likely supporter of Russian propaganda accounts with all others. Both t-tests were two-tailed, nonpaired, Welch t-tests.

computerized scoring using the resonance analysis approach. This test confirms that resonance analysis can make determinations consistent with a human analyst's judgment, even when the analyst is examining accounts 12 to 15 months more recent than the data fueling the computational analysis.

Findings: Resonance Across Time and Geography

Figure 4.2 applies our calibrated thresholds toward measuring resonance with the pro-Russia activist community in our panel sample of accounts from eight select places over a nine-month period. To count toward the vertical-axis percentages in this table, a user would need to be labeled as topic resonant and partisan resonant. Figure 4.2 suggests that tweeters from Crimea and Donetsk are much more likely to use language similar to that of known Russian propaganda disseminators. Roughly 20 percent of sampled Crimean accounts and 15 percent of sampled Donetsk accounts were labeled resonant. In contrast,

Figure 4.2
Resonance with the Pro-Russia Activist Signature

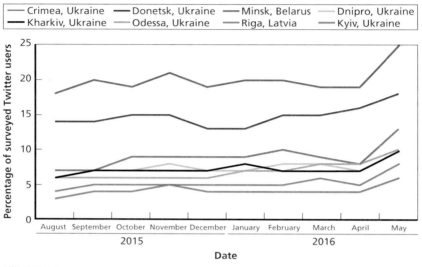

even residents of relatively pro-Russia Minsk (Belarus) barely broke 10 percent during the study period. Pro-Russia activist resonance was particularly low in places known to lean pro-Western, including Riga (Latvia) and Kyiv (Ukraine), where it generally stayed under 5 percent. Our other three Ukrainian locations (Dnipro, Kharkiv, and Odessa) tend to align more with Kyiv than Donetsk. This is likely a positive sign for Ukraine's future prospects. Within each location, resonance scores were generally stable over time. However, all places experienced a surge of pro-Russia activist resonance between April and May 2016. Most locations experienced a rise of 2 to 3 percent, but Crimea and Minsk rose 5 to 6 percent.

Summary and Implications

In conclusion, in this chapter, we tested whether we could accurately assess the linguistic affinity of a population of Twitter users for our population of pro-Russia activists identified in Chapter Three. The assumption underlying this approach was the notion that Twitter users who use the same language content patterns as a known group of partisans share in that group's ideological beliefs. In this case, we found that approximately 15 percent of users from our panels in Crimea and Donetsk share the same linguistic pattern as the pro-Russia activist Twitter community and that the rates drop as one goes farther away from the zone of pro-Russia influence. That populations highly resonant with pro-Russia activists are concentrated in such areas of strong pro-Russia influence gives the analysis a degree of validity. Also suggesting that the method is valid, our computer-generated assessments of resonance accurately correspond to the manual assessments of a blind rater.

This method could be used to assess the potential growth of this pro-Russia activist group over time. As previously noted, although we suspect that this group consists of a high number of pro-Russia bot and troll accounts, it is difficult to immediately distinguish such accounts from more-authentic conversation. Regardless, we believe that there is value in tracking the potential growth and geographic spread of this group over time. As noted in the next chapters, experts in the region report a critical need for tracking pro-Russia social media because such changes might presage pro-Russia influence and operations in the region that are more malign. To the extent that this method can detect changes across both geography and time of social media influence or activity, it could serve as a valuable tool in this endeavor.

More broadly, we believe that this method could serve as a potentially useful tool in assessing the potential impact of a variety of different propaganda sources. In Appendix C, we identified the lexical fingerprints of four different sources of Russian propaganda disseminated via Twitter. These include a sample of Russian officials, pro-Russia thought leaders, pro-Russia media, and pro-Russia trolls. Reviewing these lexical fingerprints, in and of themselves, offers value in that it highlights how Russia uses different sources to communicate different messages to different audiences. However, it is possible to use the method described above to measure the resonance of this propaganda in a population of Twitter sources.

CHAPTER FIVE

Key Challenges to Responding to the Russian Information Threat

To offer recommendations that can effectively target Russian propaganda and disinformation, we sought to identify the broader challenges affecting counterpropaganda efforts in the region. To do this, as well as to gain insights for our recommendation chapter, we interviewed more than 40 U.S. and regional experts on the Russian threat, current efforts to counter the threat, and recommendations for improving existent policy. This chapter details the challenges associated with countering Russian propaganda in the region.

Approach

We conducted interviews with key subject-matter experts and U.S., EU, and NATO officials engaged in countering Russian malign influence. First, RAND analysts conducted field travel to U.S. European Command (EUCOM) headquarters in Stuttgart, Germany, and interviewed officials in several information-relevant staff sections. We also traveled to Estonia and Latvia, where we conducted interviews with U.S. embassy personnel, host-nation security officials, journalists, and academic experts. Back in the United States, we also conducted interviews with officials at the U.S. Department of State and the Pentagon. We also conducted phone interviews with civil society experts based in Ukraine and the Baltics and officials in Ukraine.[1]

---

[1] We identified interviewees at EUCOM based on previously established contacts with the command. We identified participants in Latvia and Estonia based on earlier RAND research

Overall, we conducted more than 30 interviews. We conducted all interviews on the basis of nonattribution. RAND analysts took detailed notes during each interview and informally coded the content to enable subsequent analysis. For our analysis, we supplemented interview content with content derived from the literature.

The semistructured interview protocol used for these interviews is located in Appendix A. However, most interviews focused on three core issues:

- What threat do Russian influence efforts pose?
- What efforts are under way by the United States, international community, and host nations in countering this threat?
- What are the key challenges to countering this threat?
- What additional steps should the United States and international community undertake to better counter this threat?

Findings

History of a Shared Legacy with Russia and Modern Disenfranchisement Increase Local Russian-Language Populations' Vulnerability to Russian Messaging

The breakup of the Soviet Union in 1991 led to the creation of 15 independent countries that had formerly been Soviet republics. The impact of the Soviet period varied across countries but led to significant demographic, linguistic, and cultural changes that would have long-standing political implications, including long-standing vulnerability to Russian influence more than two decades later. In some accounts, the group of descendants of Soviet-era migrants to former Soviet countries became known as the *Russian-speaking* population (Laitin, 1998). Beyond Soviet-era migrants and their descendants, many other people in the former Soviet republics speak and understand Russian and so might be swayed or compelled by Russian-language propaganda.

---

conducted in country. We identified all remaining interview participants via the snowball method such that initial contacts recommended others within the U.S. and allied governments and with regional civil society actors.

In Estonia and Latvia, the Soviet Union engaged in a deliberate strategy of settling populations from elsewhere in the Soviet Union—primarily, but not exclusively, from Russia. The result was that, when Estonia and Latvia regained independence at the end of the Cold War, these two countries had substantial minorities of people whose families were not from Estonia or Latvia and who primarily used Russian as their native language (Kasekamp, 2010).

With the collapse of the Soviet Union, Estonia and Latvia adopted policies of legal continuity with the pre–World War II governments, which meant that people who could not trace their ancestries to pre-1940 Estonia or Latvia did not automatically gain citizenship. Nationalist movements in both countries sought to ensure that the language and culture associated with the majority population dominated the new governments, and they introduced limits on nationalization and requirements for Russian speakers to learn the majority language before they could become citizens. Noncitizens were issued identification cards that permitted work and travel within the EU. As part of the process of joining the EU, both countries liberalized their citizenship policies and made it easier for Russian speakers to gain citizenship. Still, only about half of Russian speakers in Estonia and 60 percent in Latvia had achieved citizenship by 2015 (Radin, 2017).

The socioeconomic status, political opinions, and loyalty of the Russian speakers in the Baltic states vary extensively. In both Estonia and Latvia, the Russian-speaking population is concentrated in capital cities and in regions close to the Russian border. Urban Russian speakers tend to be relatively well off, while the rural populations are, on average, in lower income brackets, although incomes in these regions still favorably compare with those in the neighboring regions in Russia. In both countries, there is a spectrum of levels of loyalty and integration into the majority society. One study in Estonia, for example, identified five categories of Russian speakers, from successfully integrated people who actively participate in Estonian society (21 percent) to an "'unintegrated' group of mainly older Russian citizens" (22 percent) (Kivirähk, 2014, pp. 8–9). Russian speakers in Latvia appeared somewhat better integrated, indicated in part by higher rates of intermarriage (Radin, 2017).

Although many Russian speakers have become well integrated, there are still political divides between the Russian-speaking and majority populations. In both Estonia and Latvia, nationalist movements remain strong, and, in both countries, there have been shifting political coalitions made up of center-right parties dominated by the majority population who are skeptical of granting additional recognition to Russian speakers. Both countries also have large political parties supported mainly by Russian speakers—Centre Party in Estonia and Harmony Centre in Latvia. Despite their relative popularity, these parties were excluded from the governing coalition political parties up until November 2016, when the Centre Party entered the Estonian governing coalition after a change in its leadership.[2]

Not unlike the Baltics, Ukraine has had a highly complex and disputed national identity—many people in the country traced their roots to Russia, the country was perhaps more closely integrated into the Soviet Union than the Baltics, and many Ukrainians were bilingual or even used Russian as their primary language.

Ukraine's ethnic composition was shaped by many factors, including human-caused demographic catastrophes, migration, and economic conditions. Specific events include the two world wars, famines, Stalin's Great Terror, forced mass deportations and resettlements, and postindependence demographic crisis (Romaniuk and Gladun, 2015). Other influential factors are the Soviet "internal colonization" and "russification" policies toward Ukraine, which, among other effects, drove the Ukrainian language from primary and higher education and made Russian dominant in highly industrialized urban areas in eastern Ukraine (Snyder, 2014). Finally, ethnic composition was influenced by changes in self-identification: Some of those who identified themselves as Russians before the collapse of the Soviet Union started identifying themselves as Ukrainians afterward (Rapawy, 1997).

As noted, the Russian language remains popular in Ukraine. According to the 2001 census, 29.6 percent defined Russian as their native language, while 67.5 percent indicated Ukrainian. In another survey, which allowed multiple choices, 54.4 percent selected Ukrai-

---

[2] Interview with technology blogger, Riga, Latvia, January 2017.

nian, 30.4 percent Russian, and 12.4 percent both Ukrainian and Russian. Other languages received less than 3 percent combined in both surveys (Khmelko, undated). Probably because of the multiethnic and multicultural environment, civic national identity in Ukraine is much stronger than ethnic national identity (Shulman, 2004; see also *Konsolidatsiya Ukrayins'koho suspil'stva*, 2016, p. 4). In addition, ties between Ukraine and Russia, albeit deeply fraught particularly under Stalin and the manufactured famine, have a lot of mutually reinforcing cleavages. For example, it is hard to find a Ukrainian family without some relatives in Russia, and vice versa.[3]

Nevertheless, a strong, anti-Russia nationalist movement emerged after the fall of the Soviet Union, although the popularity of this movement varied across the country (Shulman, 2004, pp. 64–65, 99–102). The divisions within Ukraine about its relationship with Russia and the West were brought to the fore in the 2004 Orange Revolution and 2014 Revolution of Dignity. People in western Ukraine tended to identify more often with a Western-aligned Ukrainian government and use Ukrainian as their primary language, and those in the east tended to more often use Russian and see themselves as closer to Russian. Still, even as Russian aggression in Crimea and eastern Ukraine turned many Ukrainians against Russia, they still retained their ability to understand Russian and consume Russian media.

Discriminatory Policies Against the Russian Language Enhance Disenfranchisement and Limit Opportunities for Outreach

The nationalist political influence in Estonia and Latvia further limit the potential for developing alternative media in Russia. The major Estonian and Latvian political parties that have historically dominated government oppose official recognition of the Russian language, for fear of undermining or diluting their own national culture.[4] This sen-

---

[3] Sarah Oates, Philip Merrill College of Journalism, University of Maryland, written communication, August 21, 2017.

[4] In 2015, for example, one Latvian analyst claimed that, if Russian were recognized as an official language in Latvia, the Latvian language would disappear within two generations (interview with Latvian analyst, Riga, Latvia, July 2015).

timent undermines attempts by the Latvian government, especially to develop alternatives for Russian speakers to Moscow-controlled media. The Russian-speaking mayor of Riga, Nils Ušakovs, as well as the U.S. embassy in Riga, the Latvian president, and other officials, have all been criticized for addressing the Latvian population in Russian, for example ("Latvia's Foreign Minister Asks US Embassy to Quit Using Russian Language," 2016).[5] Further, because Latvian is the official language, the Latvian government cannot fund a Russian-language station, and domestic stations must broadcast at least 65 percent of the time in Latvian. Nevertheless, Russian-language programs from Russia are easily available on cable stations (Freedom House, 2015).[6]

Estonia and Latvia have attempted to remedy the dominance of Moscow-controlled media, although with limited success because of resource and legal restrictions. A Russian-language, Estonian government–funded ETV+ went on the air in September 2015 and has been, according to one official, "a good addition" but is still under development. The intent of the station is not to compete directly with the Russian state–controlled media—rather, the station reportedly has more of a local public broadcasting approach: seeking to gain viewers by including many people in broadcasts and hoping that their friends and neighbors will watch.[7]

In the Baltics, Russian Broadcast Television and News Are the Biggest Threat

Russia-controlled TV remains a key source of entertainment and information for Russian-language populations in the Baltics. About both Latvia and Estonia, interviewees emphasized that the Russian speakers consume mainly Russian state–controlled media.[8] Many Russian speakers in Estonia and Latvia get most of their information from TV, and the most-popular stations among the Russian-speaking popula-

---

[5] Interview with government official, Riga, Latvia, January 2017.

[6] Interviews with officials and analysts, Riga, Latvia, January 2017.

[7] Interview with security official, Tallinn, Estonia, January 2017.

[8] One Latvian interviewee noted, "The speakers are in a bubble and have always been in a bubble" (interview with technology blogger, Riga, Latvia, January 2017).

tion include rebroadcasted or adapted versions of Moscow-controlled stations. Many, especially older, Russian speakers cannot easily understand TV programs in the majority language. Further, the production value and entertainment level of Moscow-funded media tend to be significantly higher, in part because of government subsidies and in part because of greater economies of scale. For example, the popular First Baltic Channel includes general entertainment, global news, and local news at a higher level of production than the Estonia- or Latvia-run local stations. Our interlocutors were seriously concerned that, because Russian speakers live in such an information cocoon, many would therefore tend to be more likely to adopt the Kremlin's perspective about current events. As one interviewee noted, non–Russia-based entertainment is "few and far between." Latvians, for example, are still "watching Russian TV because it is well funded. [Russia] gives you RT for nothing [and, with it,] you get your dollop of Russian propaganda."[9]

Threatening Social Media Content Is Often Disseminated by "Useful Idiots"

Vladimir Lenin was reported to have used the term "useful idiots" as a reference to procommunist liberals of the West who help carry out the propaganda agenda of the Russian state (Safire, 1987).[10] Today, it is used partly to refer to the various social media activists, website hosts, news sources, and others who, without direct command and control

---

[9] Phone interview with NATO official, February 2017.

[10] According to William Safire, no established citation directly attributes the phrase "useful idiots" to Lenin. One possible source comes from Yuri Annenkov, who wrote the 1966 book *Dnevnik moikh vstrech: tsikl tragedii* [People and portraits: A tragic cycle]. Annenkov was a painter and writer whom the Communist Party commissioned to do a portrait of Lenin following Lenin's death. As part of this effort, Annenkov reviewed Lenin's files, and he attributes the following quote to Lenin:

> To speak the truth is a petit-bourgeois habit. To lie, on the contrary, is often justified by the lie's aim. The whole world's capitalists and their governments, as they pant to win the Soviet market, will close their eyes to the above mentioned reality and will thus transform themselves into men who are deaf, dumb and blind. They will give us credits . . . they will toil to prepare their own suicide.

The phrase "deaf, dumb and blind," according to Safire, might be the etymology of "useful idiots."

from the Russian state, eagerly disseminate content that supports Russian propaganda aims. The active presence of such sources complicates targeting of Russian propaganda, given that it is often difficult to discriminate between authentic views and opinions on the internet and those disseminated by the Russian state.

The varied Twitter accounts identified as part of the pro-Russia activist community are a perfect example of this. These accounts certainly disseminate Russian propaganda themes and messages, but it is difficult to determine the degree to which they are "fake" troll accounts or real Twitter users engaged in genuine dialogue.

News websites, especially in Russian but also in local languages, pick up negative material about NATO and the Baltic states from Russian TV broadcasts or comments on social media pages. Such stories appear to be fake news. For example, one news story in Estonia developed from a comment page on a website stating that UK soldiers, deployed in Estonia as part of the Enhanced Forward Presence (EFP) force, acted "rudely" toward a local Estonian at a hospital. In fact, on further investigation, no UK soldiers present at the hospital in question at the time were described in the story. Security officials think (but are not certain) that this story might have been started by a fake Facebook page that presumably has Russian troll origins. In Latvia, a popular website that had previously disseminated cat videos and other benign content began disseminating content against the government of Latvia—in particular, the message that "everything is bad in Latvia." The content seemed to have the hallmarks of Russian origin; however, this does not appear to have been the actual origin. Technology blogger Jānis Polis tracked the origins of this campaign and, through investigating the registration of internet domains, found that the campaign was started by a relatively radical Russian-speaking member of the European Parliament ("Mystery Website Producer Has Ties to Harmony," year unknown).[11] In the case of the Latvian campaign, there was no clear indication that the Russian government was involved.

As the Latvian social media campaign indicates, there are significant challenges in attributing Russian-language information operations

---

[11] Interview with Latvian social media researcher.

to the Russian government. Estonian officials have similarly reported that, although they observe and monitor Russian social media, they have tracked most negative social media campaigns to disgruntled local Russian speakers. Social and economic problems that are unrelated to the presence of Russian speakers can also offer an opportunity for Russian influence. In Latvia, for example, researchers noted that Russian or pro-Russia actors tended to exploit reports of government malfeasance or conservative, antigay sentiment among the non–Russian-speaking population.[12] Although such campaigns do not necessarily directly echo Russia's own interests, they do align with Russia's general political objectives. Hence, although Russia can take advantage of the ethnic divisions within the Baltics, it also has a wide range of other tactics at its disposal.

Having Unique National Cultures in the Baltic States Makes Regional Messaging Difficult

The diversity of the three Baltic states, their small size, and the unique culture of Russian speakers also create problems for developing media that are competitive with Russia's programming. According to our interlocutors, Estonia's Russian speakers are unlikely to be receptive to Russian-language content developed for other countries—as one Estonian official explained, "No one in Estonia wants to watch Latvian television."[13] This makes it difficult to imagine a pan-Baltic or pan–former Soviet Union approach to developing alternative news media or other content. Given the small size of the Baltic states, 1.3 million in Estonia and 2.1 million in Latvia, developing sufficient scale for a campaign might therefore be difficult.

Ukraine's Approach to Information Control Might Be Difficult to Replicate

Ukraine has alternatively been able to address the popularity of Russian broadcast TV through a different tactic: censorship. In 2014, in reaction to Russian aggression and the current state of conflict with Rus-

---

[12] Interviews with analysts, Riga, Latvia, January 2017.

[13] Interview with security officials, Tallinn, Estonia, January 2017.

sian separatists, the Ukrainian government established a Ministry of Information Policy, with the mission of protecting Ukraine's informational sovereignty. The ministry was met with a lot of criticism, which emphasized risks of censorship and state propaganda, and even making parallels to George Orwell's Ministry of Truth (Miller, 2014). In 2014, Ukraine shut down broadcasts of Moscow-controlled TV.[14] The ban started from major channels in 2014 and gradually extended to include a total of 73 channels by 2016; even so, many channels are still available through satellite and internet ("V Ukrayini vzhe zaboronyly 73 rosiys'ki telekanaly" [73 Russian TV channels are already banned in Ukraine], 2016). In addition, to reduce the amount of Russian content, Ukrainian language quotas have been introduced on radio and TV. As a result, consumption of Russian TV news between 2014 and 2016 declined from 27 percent to 6 percent (InMind, 2016). And just this past year, the Ukrainian government extended this censorship policy to social media by blocking the popular Russian social media site VK ("Ukraine Bans Its Top Social Networks Because They Are Russian," 2017). Ukraine experts with whom we spoke recommended that other states in the region apply a similar tact, although European values of a free press likely mitigate against such moves.

The United States, North Atlantic Treaty Organization, and European Union Do Not Coordinate

Another challenge is the internal coordination among the U.S. government, Western government, the EU, and NATO. Within the U.S. government, the U.S. military, the State Department, the Broadcasting Board of Governors (BBG), and other agencies have a role in monitoring, analyzing, and responding to Russian influence and supporting the Baltic states. The State Department has a leading role through its management of overall U.S. foreign policy, while U.S. ambassadors

---

[14] A complete ban of media resources represents a technological challenge: Many Russian TV channels are still available through satellite signal, and there are many ways of avoiding the website ban, such as use of a virtual private network or browser add-ons. Also, because most of the TV channels are private, enforcement of a complete ban of Russian content might be challenging. In particular, capacity to produce one's own quality entertainment content in Ukraine is low, so replacing Russian content will require time and effort (Kokotyukh, 2015).

have final say over what occurs in their particular countries. A wide and growing range of State Department activities also seeks to counter the threat of Russian propaganda, including public diplomacy; the provision of local training on issues, such as media literacy; and person-to-person exchanges. The U.S. military also plays a role given its extensive resources and considerable authorities. For example, the European Reassurance Initiative provided $5.0 million in fiscal year 2017 to support the Operational Influence Platform, which is an "influence capability which leverages social media and advanced online marketing techniques to counter misinformation and propaganda by malicious actors by delivering messages through traditional, digital, and emerging media" (Office of the Under Secretary of Defense [Comptroller], 2016). In 2015 testimony, Brig Gen Charles Moore also highlighted the role of the European Reassurance military information support operations program, which provides authority to enable military information support operations teams to support partners' training and messaging (C. Moore, 2015).

Heavy-Handed Anti-Russia Messaging Could Backfire

Interviewed analysts emphasized that many Russian speakers are deeply skeptical of Western propaganda because of their experience of the Soviet Union. They might, for example, be unlikely to embrace Russian-language media that is directly produced by Western state–funded media, such as Radio Free Europe/Radio Liberty or Deutsche Welle. Other linguistic and cultural specificities of particular communities within the Baltic states will also make it difficult to effectively directly message to some populations that are most vulnerable to Russian propaganda. For example, Russian speakers in Estonia appear to use a unique dialect, which could make any Western attempt to directly communicate with Russian speakers in the country backfire. Other regions might have the same issue.

Europe is a challenging and highly politically sensitive theater for information operations. According to several regional interviews, heavy-handed or obvious U.S. "propaganda," or information activities that can be traced back to the U.S. government, could backfire and set back U.S. objectives. Political challenges, of course, confront any

U.S. government effort directing information operations at a NATO partner. In addition, although some disagreement on this point exists, several in the region note various sensitivities. One contact in Estonia noted that it is "very hard to do stuff behind the scenes here because the population is only 1.3 million." This contact noted that, for example, were the government to bring in a U.S. military information support team, "everyone would know it."[15] Likewise, a Latvia expert suggested that overt U.S. propaganda efforts might inadvertently play into Russia's own propaganda narrative.[16] Of course, not all contacts agree with these concerns, but they do suggest a need for some caution.

In addition, any messaging effort by the United States would require careful coordination between the State Department, the U.S. Department of Defense, and the intelligence community in order to ensure that any political sensitivities are addressed. One of the most-significant coordination hurdles is ensuring that a given country's U.S. ambassador approves all U.S.-initiated information campaigns. Acquiring such approval demands close coordination with the ambassador and embassy staff during the development phase of any such effort. In theory, according to the 2017 National Defense Authorization Act, the Global Engagement Center (GEC) within the State Department could take a new role leading the response to state actors, but, as of the time of this writing, the GEC's role was still developing.[17]

As multinational organizations with European members, the EU and NATO could, in theory, be best suited to respond to Russian information, but they have limited resources and difficulty formulating a coherent and organized approach. A NATO official noted that Russia had a very consistent narrative and approach but that the West, by comparison, had failed to implement a comprehensive diplomatic,

---

[15] Interview with security officials, Tallinn, Estonia, January 2017.

[16] Interview with technology blogger, Riga, Latvia, January 2017.

[17] In particular, the GEC's mandate under legislation to "lead, synchronize, and coordinate efforts of the Federal Government to recognize, understand, expose, and counter foreign state and non-state propaganda" could help alleviate some of these coordination challenges. Funding for the center to undertake its new role requires a Department of Defense decision to transfer $60 million to the State Department (Pub. L. 114-328, 2016, § 1287).

informational, military, and economic approach or coherent message. Aside from its public relations office, NATO appears to lack a capability for social media outreach. The NATO StratCom COE is a collaborative effort led by Latvia and other sponsoring nations but is relatively new. The EU, for example, initiated an effort to develop an action plan on Russia's "disinformation campaigns" in March 2015 (General Secretariat of the Council, 2015). However, its main response, the European External Action Service East StratCom effort, has only 11 people on staff. It appears difficult to imagine how the EU could develop an effective message given the complexities of the European bureaucracy and need for consensus across member states.

Summary and Implications

In summary, we identified several broad challenges that could affect the success of counterpropaganda efforts in the region. In Russia's favor lies regional "compatriots" who speak Russian, hail ancestrally from Russia, and, in some cases, have not been eagerly adopted by their resident countries. Reinforcing an observation noted in Chapter Two, Russian government broadcasts in the region serve as a potent propaganda weapon for Russia, and it is one with often relatively few regional competitors. Ukraine has addressed this problem with outright censorship, but alternative remedies will likely be necessary in the Baltics. In this media environment, it is difficult to distinguish genuine and authentic web conversation from formal Russian propaganda because Russian nonattributed content can intermix freely among like-minded activists. Finally, we note that heavy-handed anti-Russia messaging might backfire in the region given local skepticism of Western propaganda, as could the variety of dialects unique to the region.

Given these observations, it will be critical to work with local populations and media producers to create web and media content that can rival that of Russia. As previously noted, it will be critical to develop mechanisms to identify Russia propaganda content and, if necessary, help label it as such. And, of course, anti-Russia messaging will have to be conducted with care. This might mean relying on local messengers who have credibility and influence in the region. It might also require careful public relations messaging in which NATO and local governments offer genuine communications that explain policies and offer a credible alternative to alignment with Russia.

CHAPTER SIX

Recommendations

Informed in part on these observations, as well as numerous in-depth interviews with local and international experts, we have identified five key and overarching suggestions for improving the Western response to Russia's information activities against its neighbors. In the text for each recommendation, we highlight what is known about existing and related policies. These recommendations are summarized as follows:

- Highlight and "block" Russian propaganda.
- Build the resilience of at-risk populations.
- Provide an alternative to Russian information by expanding and improving local content.
- Better tell the U.S., NATO, and EU story.
- Track Russian media and develop analytic methods.

Highlight and "Block" Russian Propaganda

Numerous counter–Russian propaganda initiatives focus on exposing examples of Russian influence and fake news. In Ukraine, volunteer journalists and students eager to help identify and counter Russian propaganda on the internet have developed numerous initiatives, including Infosprotyv (information resistance), Myrotvorets (peacekeeper), and Cyber Army. One such program, StopFake, is a crowd-sourced journalism project that seeks to counter fake information about events in Ukraine. Recent headlines, for example, refute published stories that deceptively claim that that German Chancellor Angela Merkel was ending Russian sanctions or that Ukraine's credit rating was falling. Both of these stories were published on Russian news outlets ("Fake: Merkel for Ending Russian Sanctions," 2017; see also "Fake: Ukraine's Falling Credit Rating," 2017). The website also offers broader information articles on the state of Russian propaganda, such as a story on Russian propaganda emanating out of Bulgaria (Vatsov and Iakimova, 2017).

The EU East StratCom Task Force likewise seeks to expose Russian propaganda. The task force has three key objectives: (1) Better communicate EU policies in eastern European countries and countries east of Europe, (2) support independent media in the region, and (3) raise awareness of Russia's information campaign. The task force disseminates its analysis via its website and a weekly email newsletter. Appendix B provides an analysis of content from this newsletter for the weeks of December 13, 2016; December 20, 2016; and January 12, 2017 ("Disinformation Review Issue 51," 2016; "Disinformation Review Issue 52," 2016; "Disinformation Review Issue 53," 2017). One representative of the task force observed that its key goal was awareness:

> [W]here we started in September 2015, it was depressing because it looked like 95 percent of Brussels didn't believe in Russian propaganda and [the] other 5 percent said it was not a big threat. Now it is a different situation, and most [of] Brussels [sees it as a threat.] We see [that] the interest in this issue is on the rise and more media are writing about it; more member states taking action. . . . We are working for these objectives. We try to raise awareness, make it a theme of public debate. We are still not there but moving in this direction.[1]

Although such efforts to highlight Russian disinformation should be lauded, we observe at least two key limitations. The first is speed. By the time examples of Russian disinformation are highlighted, the information has likely already reached and possibly influenced key at-risk audiences. Second, the audiences most at risk of being influenced

---

[1] Phone interview with European official, February 2017.

by Russian disinformation might be the least likely to routinely consume or access disinformation sites. Consequently, new approaches, possibly taking advantage of advances in modern information technology, might be needed to effectively counter Russian propaganda. We highlight several potential applications.

First, various technology firms, including Facebook, have initiated some efforts to address fake news. Facebook, for example, has developed a "disputed tag" that warns users that online fact-checkers or Facebook's own algorithms have identified the content as suspect. Google offers a Fact Check tag that it applies to suspect content displayed on the Google News portal. Neither Facebook nor Google labels the stories as true or false. Twitter, alternatively, offers its verified-account system. Essentially, an account that has been vetted to ensure that it represents whom it says it does receives a blue check mark next to the account name (Twitter, undated). These efforts by Google and Facebook represent a start in combating fake news; however, the extent to which these initiatives capture Russian-promulgated content remains to be seen. As for Twitter, offering an opportunity for users to verify accounts is likely different from and not as effective as terminating accounts known as trolls or automated bot accounts of Russian origin.

Second, taking a lesson from a counterextremism program, Ross Frenett of the firm Moonshot CVE argues that Google Ads might provide an alternative effort to counter Russian propaganda.[2] One counter–violent extremism program, the Redirect Method, has received significant attention in the press as being a potentially effective approach to reducing the appeal of the Islamic State. Taking advantage of the technology behind Google AdWords, this method identifies potential ISIS recruits through their Google searches and exposes them to curated YouTube videos debunking ISIS recruiting themes. In one pilot experiment, the method was able to reach 320,906 people by exposing them to a total of 500,070 minutes of counterextremist videos (Redirect Method, undated). To apply this method to Russian propaganda, it might be possible to use Google AdWords to identify instances in which people search Google about particular fake-news

---

[2]   Interview with Ross Frenett, Moonshot CVE, Washington, D.C., June 26, 2017.

stories or other Russian propaganda themes. These people could then be exposed to information that disputes such stories or otherwise exposes them to alternative news or video content.

Third, we previously noted that Russian trolls have used comment sections in various news articles to promote their messages in nonattributed ways. Two mechanisms might be available to reduce such trolling. First, news and other organizations could require Facebook authentication for those people seeking to contribute to the organization's website comment section. To create an account, Facebook requires that a prospective user use the user's real name, and the organization can, with some success, ferret out those who attempt to sign up with fake names. Consequently, requiring Facebook authentication for contributing to a comment page might limit the degree to which an actor, such as Russia, can use anonymous troll farms to take over the page. Recent research also shows that it might reduce the presence of malign and hostile content (A. Moore, 2016). A second potential technology, called Perspective, has been developed by Jigsaw, a technology incubator at Alphabet, Google's parent company. Jigsaw created a machine learning tool that identifies toxic and incendiary comments that can then be queued up for review and potential elimination by comment forum moderators. *The New York Times*, for example, uses the tool to help its moderators identify abusive online comments ("The Times Is Partnering with Jigsaw to Expand Comment Capabilities," 2016). Jigsaw has made the code for Perspective widely available and is looking to expand the capability to the Russian language, in which it might then be applied to counter state-sponsored trolling (Greenberg, 2017).

Finally, as previously noted, Russia systematically uses nonattributed social media accounts in the form of trolls and automated social media bots to conduct its information campaign. Several academic and news articles illustrate the extent of this campaign that targets social media users not only in the Baltics and Ukraine but also in Europe and the United States (Goldsberry, Goldsberry, and Sharma, 2015).

It is critical that the United States monitor this campaign closely and identify and track the nonattributed social media accounts employed as part of the campaign. A key question is how to counter such a campaign. One approach is to attempt to "out" these accounts by publicizing their sources. Joshua Goldsberry of the tech analytic firm Alqimi National Security, has cataloged the nature of this campaign by analyzing Russian troll accounts and their U.S.-directed hashtag campaigns on Twitter. One approach that Goldsberry offers is to openly publish this list of troll accounts (Goldsberry, Goldsberry, and Sharma, 2015). On Twitter, this could include sending out retweets or mentions that publicize the user's deceptive and malicious nature. And to the extent that trolls participate in a malicious hashtag campaign, such as the #ColumbianChemicals hoax, government accounts would be able to post a correction directly using the same hashtag. Authorities can also identify such accounts to social media companies that might be able to terminate the accounts based on terms-of-service violations. In particular, the most-influential bot and troll accounts should be prioritized for such terms-of-service violations.

Build the Resilience of At-Risk Populations

Building the resilience of at-risk populations focuses on helping Russian colinguists and others in the former Soviet states better identify fake news and other Russia-authored content that has a clear propagandist intent. Numerous experts in Estonia, Latvia, and Ukraine made such recommendations, which focus on media literacy training.[3] Observed a private-sector expert in digital communications, "The first thing I would do is invest a lot of money in media literacy training. [E]very other way is [just] two propaganda wars moving against each

---

[3] The Center for Media Literacy, a U.S.-based educational program, notes on its website that media literacy

> helps young people acquire an empowering set of "navigational" skills which include the ability to: Access information from a variety of sources. Analyze and explore how messages are "constructed" whether through social media, print, verbal, visual or multimedia. Evaluate media's explicit and implicit messages against one's own ethical, moral and/or democratic principles. Express or create their own messages using a variety of media tools, digital or not. Participate in a global media culture. (Center for Media Literacy, undated)

other."[4] Another activist noted, "Pointing out Russian propaganda is not so helpful, but [it is] helpful to help people understand [that] there are untruths. . . . Critical thinking and education [are important]."[5] Although strengthening the overall education system will prove critical to enhancing basic media literacy skills, we highlight several specific recommendations for media literacy training.

Some such efforts in eastern Europe are currently under way. For example, the NGO Baltic Centre for Media Excellence, with some international funding, provides training to journalists in the Baltics and conducts media literacy training in the region. In addition to helping journalists avoid becoming "unwitting multipliers of misleading information," the organization works with schoolteachers in the region to help them "decode media and incorporate media research into teaching." The center also works to guide schoolchildren with media production programs and help raise awareness of fake news on social media.[6] In addition, the U.S. embassy in Latvia is looking to initiate media literacy programming. A local tech entrepreneur in Latvia is interested in creating an NGO start-up that would advocate for broader media literacy training and develop a Baltic-focused crowd-sourced fact-checking website along the lines of the popular English-language fact-checking site Snopes ("About Snopes.com," undated).

Beyond these disparate efforts, establishing media literacy training as part of a national curriculum could be critical. Such is the recommendation of Tessa Jolls, director of the Center for Media Literacy, a Los Angeles–based NGO.[7] She argues that such training has been proven effective and is increasingly critical in an information-empowered age. Both Canada and Australia have developed such curricula. In addition, Sweden, out of concern about Russian fake news and propaganda, has also launched a nationwide school program to

---

[4]   Interview with technology blogger, Riga, Latvia, January 2017.

[5]   Phone interview with Baltic media expert, January 2017.

[6]   Phone interview with Baltic media expert, January 2017.

[7]   Phone interview with Tessa Jolls, director, Center for Media Literacy, July 7, 2017.

teach students to identify Russian propaganda (Priest and Birnbaum, 2017).

In addition, Jolls, recognizing that a curriculum-based training program will take time to develop and establish impact, recommends that authorities launch a public information campaign that teaches the concepts of media literacy to a mass audience. This campaign, disseminated via conventional and new media, could be targeted to the populations in greatest need. It is likewise possible to meld a public information campaign with social media–driven training programs. Facebook has also launched its own media literacy campaign, most recently marked by distributing a set of tips to users for spotting fake-news stories. This has been publicized in the UK ahead of the upcoming parliamentary elections.[8] It would certainly be possible to develop such programs for an eastern European and Ukrainian audience.

Expand and Improve Local and Original Content

Several respondents interviewed for this study raised the question of whether it is necessary to counter Russian propaganda or to compete with it. A national security researcher in Latvia raised this question. This researcher argued that, to "counter something" is to "follow" and, in that instance, "you are already losing."[9] To effectively compete, others argue, is to develop content that can displace the pro-Russia narrative. One interlocutor with whom we spoke put it this way:

> Our approach is more, "yes, you have Russian-speaking minorities, and, yes, it is true [that] there is propaganda from Russia," but why are these people receptive to this? Why are they listening to the Kremlin narrative? The simple answer is [that] there is no alternative. Most speak only Russian; they are not integrated into Estonian [and] Latvian societies; they are alienated and isolated; and all they can do is watch TV shows coming out of Russia.

---

[8]   These tips include "Be skeptical of headlines," "Look closely at the URL [uniform resource locator]," and "Investigate the source" (Sulleyman, 2017).

[9]   Interview with analyst, Riga, Latvia, January 2017.

Our approach was to strengthen the local independent Russian-language media.[10]

Ukraine and its Ministry of Information Policy have also taken a slightly similar approach by supporting the creation of an Information Army—an online platform to unite volunteers who wish to help fight Russian propaganda. According to news reports, more than 40,000 volunteers have joined. Overall effectiveness and impact of the ministry and its initiatives still need to be assessed (Sharkov, 2015).

Informed by our conversations abroad and in Washington, we have identified four specific recommendations for increasing alternative content in a region that otherwise receives a heavy dose of Russian state–sponsored programming. And given the importance of affecting the entire media environment, we should note that these recommendations for alternative content span both new and old media alike (Smyth and Oates, 2015).

Empower Influencers on Social Media

Commercial marketers use brand ambassador programs to identify key influencers within their fan bases and then empower them through a series of engagements that seek to enhance their social media skills and connect them with sharable content. This approach is premised on the fact that such influencers already have an established audience and that they are viewed as more credible, in large part because of their independence, than, say, a brand's paid advertisements. We have recently published a report documenting how such brand ambassador campaigns could be used to support ISIS opponents who are influential on Twitter (Helmus and Bodine-Baron, 2017). A similar program could be applied in the near-Russia region (and elsewhere) to identify and assist pan-European Russian-language influencers on social media (e.g., YouTube stars, Twitterati).

Such an approach received broad support among those we interviewed. Representatives at the StratCom COE talk about supporting an "army of elves" who can create a "bubble of positive messaging."

---

[10] Phone interview with civil-society expert, January 2017.

"The more supporters on our side," they observe, "the bigger the bubble of positive messaging. If you have more supporters on your side, you can expect to grow even faster and [have more] influence."[11] A NATO official agrees and notes that such an approach has a unique appeal for NATO, which is otherwise barred from attempting to use psychological operations on its own people and cannot disseminate nonattributed products.

> A lot of problem we have is [that] we should be getting others to carry weight for us. The best person to argue [with] the Russians in Latvia, it is a Russian in Latvia saying they are ok. We need to target people [who] have credibility, and we need to support them.[12]

Other interviewed Ukrainian activists agree.

Some of this work is under way already, although the organization engaged in this work asked that it not be cited or directly named in our report. In articulating its approach, however, its representative stated that its goal is to identify social media influencers who speak Russian but have a "pan-European identity":

> Only because you speak Russian does not mean you support the Kremlin. Loads of Russian speakers are living in the Baltics [but they are] not politically Russian. . . . So there is a real opportunity to strengthen their voice and have them represent the idea that there is a Russian-speaking European identity. You can believe in the value of NATO, European Union, and liberal democracy and still speak Russian. [Use] these guys to [support] that opinion and make them representative of local Russian-speaking minorities. That is [the] fundamental idea behind that approach.[13]

This is the concept that underlies the findings reported in Chapter Three. In that chapter, we used community detection algorithms,

---

[11] Interview with NATO StratCom COE staff, January 2017.

[12] Phone interview with NATO official, February 2017.

[13] Phone interview with civil-society expert, January 2017.

combined with lexical analysis, to identify a relatively large and highly influential community of pro-Ukraine/anti-Russia activists, as well as pro-Russia/anti-Ukraine propagandists. We also identified relevant fence-sitter communities that are connected to the pro-Ukraine activists but have not yet been galvanized to participate in the anti-Russia fight. Applying various measures of centrality that can assess the relative influence of individual accounts would make identifying key accounts that are influential among associated fence-sitter communities relatively straightforward. Organizations seeking to counter Russian propaganda can then seek to work with these accounts to enhance their influence potential.

What does this process of working with influencers look like? Applying a brand ambassador model to this community would mean identifying and reaching out to influential users and establishing a trusted relationship. In-person or online training programs could be used to help these people more effectively utilize social media (and offline communication techniques) to communicate their pro-Ukraine message. Efforts could also be undertaken to connect these users to better social media content and to inform their efforts with powerful social media analytics.[14]

Of course, this could expand beyond just the pro-Ukraine activist community. Indeed, such brand ambassador programs could be used with influencers across a variety of social media channels. It could also target other prominent experts, such as academics, business leaders, and other potentially prominent people. Authorities must ultimately take care in implementing such a program given the risk that contact with U.S. or NATO authorities might damage influencer reputations. Engagements must consequently be made with care, and, if possible, government interlocutors should work through local NGOs. In addition, those managing influencer engagement programs should not seek to unduly influence an influencer's messaging content. Influencers maintain their credibility because of their independence; sometimes, this independence leads them to communicate content that does not fit the preferred message of a brand manager or government or NGO

---

[14] For a thorough description of the model, see Helmus and Bodine-Baron, 2017.

interlocutor. In such instances, efforts to control the character of this content can often do more harm than good.

Fund Content Creation

Current efforts are under way to support the creation of alternative media content. There is an international initiative to develop a creative content hub in which international donors will donate to a basket fund that will pay a committee of local experts who will, in turn, manage and distribute the money to Russian-language producers and broadcasters that pitch various projects. Argued the influencer marketer in the region, "With that money, you will produce and fund a ton more Russian-language content across the region."[15] Another interviewee from the region suggested that "like-minded donors" can come together and recommended a content-creation fund and can commission work.[16] Funding Russian-language and local media creators gives the work a local level of relevance that foreign broadcasters cannot achieve.[17]

Train Russian-Language Journalists

A related approach is to support journalism training in the Baltic region and Ukraine. We asked an Estonian security official how the international community can help counter Russian influence. He recommended the promotion of a "higher standard of journalism" in the region, noting that journalism training "would be helpful, especially for the online community."[18] Such recommendations were repeated in numerous conversations with regional experts.

Several such efforts have been ongoing. For example, the United States sponsored a TechCamp in the region that brought together local journalists from eastern Europe and offered a several-day training program that also included a sponsored yearlong investigative project.

---

[15] Phone interview with civil-society expert, January 2017.

[16] Phone interview with Baltic media expert, January 2017.

[17] Phone interview with Baltic media expert, January 2017.

[18] Interview with security officials, Tallinn, Estonia, January 2017.

Such an approach appears valuable, although it would need to be operated on a more sustained basis. More significantly, the Baltic Centre for Media Excellence provides various training opportunities for journalists and local media outlets in the Baltics. In some cases, this training takes the form of a sustained mentorship. For one local newspaper in Latvia, the center spent a week with the editors and journalists and offered follow-up sessions. It also conducts small and targeted training efforts, such as a half-day effort on digital strategies, depending on the needs of the outlet or journalist.[19]

One challenge, however, with such trainings is the lack of effective media outlets in the region. Using eastern Latvia media outlets as an example, one expert noted that the media outlets are "very weak," are often politically affiliated, or have "little local oligarchs that control them." She continued, "It is a mess in terms of journalism. And they don't provide viable alternatives to Russian channels. Investing in existing media that are corrupt and low quality is a waste of money."[20] Consequently, one goal is to help trained journalists find alternative places to work. One expert in the region talked of supporting a start-up hub in the region that could attract and keep trained local Russian-language journalists. Such efforts, however, will require outside start-up funding and careful training and mentorship to enable such hyperlocal media initiatives to become self-sustaining. An alternative would be to support digital media hubs.[21] The expert continued, "If you develop new ideas in digital environment, that is easier than with TV channel or a newspaper."[22] An alternative would be to help journalists start their

---

[19] Phone interview with Baltic media expert, January 2017.

[20] Phone interview with Baltic media expert, January 2017. Another expert in the region noted, "The risk is that, even with effective training, journalists lack access to a platform that is independent, and so they fall back to [a] media environment that is influenced by politics."

[21] This expert elaborated:

> Training on one weekend a month covers all the different topics [and] helps you interact with different media actors. After this training, which is step 1, if you give great training, they will ask, "where are all the platforms?" So level 2, hyperlocal media platforms . . . need to figure out other [platforms to disseminate content]. (phone interview with civil-society expert, January 2017)

[22] Phone interview with Baltic media expert, January 2017.

own social media channels with projects funded through a content-creation hub, as discussed in the previous section.

Increase Russian-Language Programming

Another alternative is to directly support Russian-language TV programming in the region. This is the approach undertaken by the Estonians who supported the creation of a Russian-language public access TV station called ETV+. The station first aired on September 28, 2015. It broadcasts in both Estonian and Russian languages, and it is intended to provide the Russian minority living in Estonia access to a broadcast channel that is not controlled by Russia. In Latvia, local TV station LTV-7 offers some programming in the Russian language but, by law, must offer Latvian programming as well.

The Ukrainians too have taken this approach. One of the first initiatives of the Ukrainian Ministry of Information Policy was a launch of a global International Broadcasting Multimedia Platform of Ukraine (UA|TV) channel with objective information about Ukraine to dismantle fakes created by Russian propaganda. The channel broadcasts online at its own website (UA|TV, undated), on YouTube, on several European cable networks, and through three satellites in five languages (Ukrainian, Russian, English, Arabic, and Qırımtatarca, the language of Crimean Tatars). Insufficient funding and the need to build audience in a competitive environment are the key challenges for the UA|TV project (Nekrasov, 2016).

Finally, the BBG produces and airs *Current Time*, a 24-hour Russian-language TV network that seeks to address the "needs of Russian-speaking audiences in Russia, Central and Eastern Europe, and around the world" by offering "professional, objective and trustworthy news and information" that can serve as a counterweight to Russia's RT and Sputnik (BBG, 2017). *Current Time* also airs documentary programming and reportedly complements its TV programming with digital content. Ultimately, the degree to which *Current Time* gains a broad following is an empirical question, and the BBG is conducting surveys to assess market penetration outside Russia. However, as an article in *The Economist* notes, in May, *Current Time* videos were viewed 40 million times online ("America's Answer to Russian

Propaganda TV," 2017). It would certainly be a positive development if *Current Time* could draw viewers away from Russian TV programming of RT and Sputnik. One effort that might assist in this regard is expanding programming to include more conventional entertainment programming.

There are reportedly plans for *Current Time* to air travel, cooking, and other entertainment programs. Highlighting the value of such a move, one U.S. embassy staffer from the region, for example, gave the example of the U.S. situation comedy *Will and Grace* and the importance this program had on influencing national opinions about the gay and lesbian community. She observed,

> That is really important and has values. It is also something that could be done that is not country specific. It could be any kind of Russian diaspora community. It could be done in a way [that communicates] Western values, and it could be interesting enough for folks to watch.[23]

In addition, it might be noted that such programming is so transparent that it can avoid the risks that might otherwise be associated with propaganda campaigns.

Better Tell the U.S., North Atlantic Treaty Organization, and European Union Story

Much of the Russian propaganda efforts in the region are focused on driving a wedge between Russian-language populations and former Soviet states in which they live, as well as with NATO and the EU. Beyond "countering" these messages in a tit-for-tat way, it will likely be critical for the United States, NATO, and the EU to offer their own messages that offer a compelling argument for populations to align with the West.

---

[23] Phone interview with U.S. official, March 2017.

Support Enhanced Forward Presence with Effective Public Relations
Consider NATO's EFP in eastern Europe. To provide a deterrent against threatening Russian actions in eastern Europe, NATO has deployed battalion-sized battle groups to Estonia, Latvia, Lithuania, and Poland. Experts in the region note that Russia already seeks to use this presence to enhance Russian speakers' suspicions toward Europe and NATO. A potential example of this affect on social media is of the previously noted viral fake story of UK soldiers harassing an elderly woman in an Estonian hospital.

Security experts in Estonia and Latvia urge that proper efforts be undertaken to ensure integration of NATO's presence in eastern Europe. One approach that has apparently paid dividends is civil engagement activities conducted on the part of EFP forces. In Latvia, for example, U.S. soldiers have reportedly conducted numerous civil engagements with the local populations. In one example, soldiers cut firewood for local Russian-speaking Latvians. Locals were reportedly overheard saying, "A Russian soldier wouldn't do that."[24] In another instance, U.S. soldiers conducted a well-received event in eastern Estonia, showing local citizens their equipment and trucks.

In addition to such events, it will also be critical to support the EFP forces with effective communication. As one NATO expert observed,

> The first thing we need to do is make sure the host nation understands wants and supports [the EFP]. [It's] not that hard a task in Estonia, Latvia, and Lithuania, [but] you still have 30 percent of [the population] who are Russian sympathetic if not pro-Russian. They need to understand who we are, why we are there, and . . . that we are part of their team and [they are part of ours].[25]

NATO will consequently need to support EFP forces with messaging that effectively communicates the intent and purpose behind the forces and that reassures concerned local populations. Efforts that support EFP civil engagement activities with compelling video and

---

[24] Interview with U.S. officials, Riga, Latvia, January 2017.

[25] Phone interview with NATO official, February 2017.

other sharable content might also be valuable. And NATO should likewise provide support and training, where needed, to local public affairs and other communication personnel. Local government and military public affairs personnel can play their part in creating and disseminating entertaining and sharable content that supports the EFP mission. There might also be value in working with selected Russian-language journalists and even citizen bloggers and social media activists whose reporting on EFP exercises and events might prove particularly credible among Russian-speaking audiences.

Offer a Clear and Convincing Strategic Message

More broadly than messaging EFP forces or other NATO activities, there is a need to offer skeptical Russian speakers in the Baltics and Ukraine a compelling vision for siding with the West. It might be that liberal democracies no longer sell themselves or at least it is a more difficult sell when confronted with a fire hose of contradictory content. In the Baltics, for example, this means that NATO and the EU need to craft a message around the benefits or value of EU and NATO membership. As one NATO official highlighted, "When you look at the Russian social media effort, [you see a] huge amount of effort to tell [the Ukrainians] that Ukraine is a shit hole and that it is better to be in the Russian orbit." He argued, "The EU piece of the puzzle is to show citizens of their own country that this is a good place to be." He further recommended that, like any good marketing message, the NATO or EU message be focused and clear: "The best way to defeat Russian propaganda is to have clear and consistent and entertaining narrative of our own. . . . If you are sure about your argument, if you project image of clarity, then you can withstand a lot of rubbish."[26] The advice seems sound. It is an impossible task to effectively correct all fake-news stories maligning the Baltics or Ukraine and their relationships with the West. To the extent that the West, including the EU, the United States, and NATO, can tell its story in a clear and convincing manner, that might make Russia's job at propaganda that much harder. Each nation in the region should likewise make concerted efforts to speak to Russian lin-

---

[26] Phone interview with NATO official, February 2017.

guists living in that country and clearly articulate how and why that nation offers them a brighter future.

Track Russian Media and Develop Analytic Methods

To effectively counter Russian propaganda, it will be critical to track Russian influence efforts. The information requirements are varied and include the following:

- Identify fake-news stories and their sources.
- Understand narrative themes and content that pervade various Russian media sources.
- Understand the broader Russian strategy that underlies tactical propaganda messaging.

It will also be important to identify and track the identities and influence of unattributed Russian social media accounts that take the form of bots or trolls. These accounts represent a potentially pernicious form of influence and one that has been targeted against audiences in eastern Europe and Ukraine but also in the United States.

Monitoring various social media channels in the Baltics and Ukraine will also be important as a way of identifying any Russian shaping campaign that could prelude more-aggressive political or military action. As one Pentagon-based expert observed, "If you saw them spike their efforts in the Baltics, then you know something is happening."[27] Another at State asked, "How can we use these tools to predict and spot trends? When is the boiling point that we need to pay attention?"[28] Such views align nicely with that of the Estonians, who themselves fear that increased Russian social media operations could serve as a prelude to mischief.

This study did not seek to conduct a comprehensive analysis of U.S. and allied efforts to monitor Russian propaganda on social media

---

[27] Interview with Pentagon official, Washington, D.C., February 2017.

[28] Interview with U.S. State Department officials, January 2017.

or via any other channel. Thus, it is impossible to attest to the degree to which effective monitoring mechanisms are put in place. We know of several ongoing efforts. In addition to NGOs, such as StopFake, the EU's East StratCom Task Force publishes information on Russian propaganda efforts. Estonian security officials, for example, report that they routinely monitor Russian media efforts. And EUCOM has recently worked to gain contracted support to conduct social media monitoring and analysis. In addition, the NATO StratCom COE, based in Riga, Latvia, drafts varied research papers on a host of strategic communication topics confronting NATO, including studies on Russian propaganda.

However, we were generally surprised at the number of security organizations that lacked situational awareness of Russian social media and other propaganda campaigns. As one representative of a critical EU organization observed,

> I personally find the most scary thing that we are the unit that should know the most about this issue in Europe: We do not know how many disinformation channels, how many directly or indirectly, how many messages spread per day, how many people they reach, how many people believe in disinformation messaging. We have only nonspecific opinion polls.[29]

Ultimately, it will be key for different members of relevant U.S. agencies, as well as NATO, EU, and key nations in eastern Europe, to ensure that they have effective mechanisms in place to identify and understand the nature of Russian propaganda. This might include working with relevant technology firms to ensure that contracted analytic support is available. Contracted support is reportedly valuable because technology to monitor social media data is continually evolving, and such firms can provide the expertise to help identify and analyze trends, and they can more effectively stay abreast of the changing systems and develop new models as they are required.[30] There is also

---

[29] Phone interview with EU official, February 2017.

[30] Interview with U.S. official, Stuttgart, Germany, January 2017.

talk of the United States offering broader support to the StratCom COE. One U.S. official observed that it is a "great think tank" and suggested that the United States would be well served to contribute U.S. analysts to the international body. He suggested that doing so would "signal U.S. support for this group" and help shape the group's agenda: "It would be powerful."[31]

Finally, we observe that the analytic approach identified in Chapter Four provides at least one framework for tracking the impact and spread of Russian influence. Additional approaches will need to be developed and refined as Russia's methods evolve. Chapter Four describes an approach that develops a linguistic fingerprint of a propaganda source—in this case, that of the pro-Russia activist group—and then scans a longitudinal panel of Twitter users in the region to identify the number of accounts with Twitter content that represents a statistical match to the fingerprint. This then allows one to track the potential spread and adoption of that propaganda across both time and geography. If the pro-Russia activist group is indeed constituted with a high percentage of Russia-managed bot and troll accounts, the method could serve as a tool to assess the spread of these accounts, which might, in turn, serve as a potential indicator and warning for Russian influence operations.

---

[31] Interview with Pentagon official, Washington, D.C., February 2017.

Additional Technical Details

This appendix lists additional technical details related to lexical and resonance analysis.

Text Regularization

To enhance the signal-to-noise ratio for lexical and resonance analysis, it is important to first standardize text. In particular, for all of the analyses in this report, we performed the following steps:

1. Remove punctuation outside of that that serves a special language function (such as hyphenated terms). Protect #hashtags, @usernames, and web links from cleaning.
2. Remove all letters outside the common letters of the targeted language. That is to say, constrain the character set to select Unicode characters in the U+0400 through U+045F Cyrillic block. Allow selected characters from the U+0020 through U+007E Latin Unicode block because of its importance for specifying, for example, usernames and numeric values. Some study designs might wish to relax this constraint, in order to capture emoji. Resonance analysis can support this, but our advice is to be conservative in how many total characters are allowed.
3. Regularize spacing and capitalization.
4. Remove extremely rare words (appearing less than once per 100 million words or three times total in the baseline corpus) and ubiquitous words (appearing more often than once per

10,000 words in the baseline corpus). The 100 million and 10,000 bounds are not immutable; specific applications might require modifying the range somewhat. The important point is to remove overly rare or overly common terms.

5. Stem the language to remove all conjugation, diacritics, and similar features. The language stemmed is based on Twitter's categorization of the language used in the tweet.

Detector Calibration

An ideal threshold must be *calibrated* so that it delivers a high true positive rate while keeping false positives to a minimum. Using network analysis, we identified two communities that discussed targeted topics at an elevated rate, of which one consisted primarily of pro-Russia Twitter accounts. We used these communities to calibrate our thresholds, as described in this section.

Figure A.1 displays the calibration data for the topic-resonance score (propensity to talk about topics that members of the pro-Russia activist and pro-Ukraine activist communities discuss). The thresholds (shown on the horizontal axis) are standard deviations above the topic-resonance scores that we might expect to see by chance alone, given how often topic signature words appear in the tweets of our baseline population. So, for example, a detection threshold of 1.2 indicates that a user is considered to be topic resonant if that user's score was at least 1.2 standard deviations above the average topic-resonance score for people in the baseline population. The vertical axis indicates the percentage of users in a particular category who qualified as topic resonant at a given threshold.

Using these data, we identified 0.5 standard deviations as an appropriately conservative threshold. At this threshold, about 80 percent of known pro-Ukraine activists are labeled topic resonant, and just under 70 of known pro-Russia activists. In the process, we also labeled 23 percent of the baseline population as topic resonant. This percentage is elevated, but not unreasonably so, because the conflict in

Figure A.1
Topic-Resonance Detection Calibration

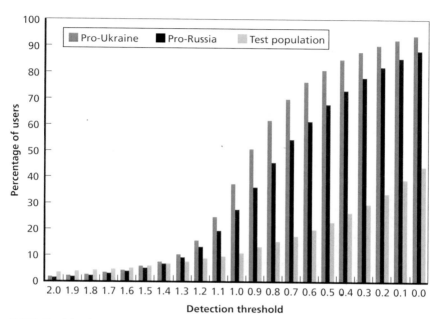

NOTE: The blue bars indicate the percentage of members in the pro-Ukraine activist community who were labeled topic resonant at a given threshold. The black bars indicate the percentage of members in the pro-Russia activist community who were labeled topic resonant at a given threshold. The gold bars report the percentage of the baseline general population labeled topic resonant at that threshold. A well-calibrated threshold should mark most known partisans as resonant but should not mark most of the general population as topic resonant in the process.
RAND *RR2237-A.1*

Ukraine and Russia's actions in the region received significant media coverage during this period and were widely discussed on Twitter.

Figure A.2 displays the calibration data for the partisan-resonance score. As with the previous figure, the horizontal axis indicates the detection threshold, and the vertical axis indicates the percentage of users in a particular category who would be labeled as partisan resonant at that threshold.

Figure A.2
Partisan-Resonance Detection Calibration

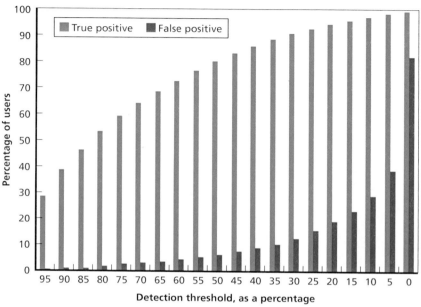

The two categories correspond to our two groups of known partisans. The green bars (true positive) indicate the percentage of known pro-Russia activists who would be labeled as partisan resonant at a given threshold. The red bars (false positive) indicate the percentage of known pro-Ukraine activists labeled as partisan resonant with the Russian propaganda signature. Because this signature is specifically designed to distinguish between these two groups, an ideal threshold is one at which all pro-Russia activists but no pro-Ukraine activists are labeled partisan resonant. Because we would rather underestimate than overestimate, we set a goal of keeping the false positive rate under 5 percent and chose a threshold of 60 percent. At this threshold, 4 percent of pro-Ukraine activist accounts are falsely labeled as partisan resonant with Russian propaganda, but 73 percent of pro-Russia activist accounts are correctly labeled.

Additional Community Lexical Characterization

This appendix details the analytic findings pertaining to other communities in our data set. We chose these communities for analysis based on their large size or high centrality in the community network (or both). For the most part, size was highly correlated with centrality, but a few with fewer than 10,000 users were surprisingly central and so were included in the analysis.

Because our data were not restricted by topic, many of these communities are extraneous to the conversation about the Ukraine–Russia conflict, but, because they are still connected to those accounts and communities that are discussing that conflict and spreading propaganda, they add some value and context to the overall analysis, and we include them here for completeness.

Community 1040: Apolitical Belarusians

Community 1040 is part of the more political metacommunity, contains 17,207 users, and consists mostly of Belarusian accounts and topics. Overpresent locations include Belarus and cities in Belarus—Minsk, Gomel, and Brest. Overpresent personal accounts belong to Belarusians, covering domestic issues and events related to Belarus. Overpresent words are related to domestic topics—*Belarus, government, Lukashenko* (Alexander Lukashenko, president of Belarus). Underpresent terms include *propaganda* and terms related to events in Ukraine. Discussion themes focus on news and events related to Belarus, and frequent topics include work, sports, weather, travel, technology, and show business. Politics and propaganda (*Lukashenko, Putin,* and *Novorossiya*) are mentioned in the context of formal news reports, sometimes in a sarcastic manner.

Community 1049: Gadgets and Life Hacks

Community 1049, part of the more political metacommunity, is an apolitical community, focused on tech and gadgets, as well as humor and cat pics, with 29,776 users. It is probably similar to community 54 in metacommunity 1025. Overpresent accounts are dedicated to technology, gadgets, life hacks, humor, sports, and business (@macdigger_ru, @ru_lh, @4pdaru, and @iphones_ru). This community probably includes a mix of Ukrainians and Russians; there is a significant number of overpresent Ukrainian words: ти (you), дуже (very), як (how). Overpresent geographic terms include some Ukrainian cities and regions—*Sumy, Luhansk, Zakarpattya,* and *Mykolaiv.* Terms related to propaganda—*Russia, USA, Crimea, Donbass, NATO,* and *Maidan*—are all underpresent, as are #news and accounts of news agencies. Personal pronouns and curse words are overpresent, indicating that a significant part of the content is probably original human tweets and lively discussions. Discussion themes represent a broad range of interests; most frequent are tech, gadgets, iPhones, Xboxes, life hacks, humor, and business. Events and propaganda around Ukraine, Russia, Donbass, and Crimea are mostly ignored. Putin and Poroshenko are presented in a neutral way, mostly in the context of official news reports.

Community 1117: Celebrities and Show Business

Community 1117, part of the more politically oriented metacommunity, is apolitical, and its 33,864 members are interested in entertainment and TV shows. Overpresent accounts include those of Ukrainian child internet stars and focus on Russian pop culture: @uazhenyas, @blessedatworld, and @ksuntatyana. Overpresent hashtags in this community include #tv, #showbusiness, #review, #tvguide,

#watch, #youtube, #video, and #fashion. One overpresent hashtag is #newsCrimea, but its content is very neutral, with only local daily news and no geopolitics. The TV channels that are most frequently mentioned are those that are watched in most post-Soviet countries, with entertainment-only content: CTC and TNT. Geographic terms are fairly broad and include *Germany, France, Russia, Ukraine, USA, Turkey, Moscow, Crimea*, and many Ukrainian cities, mostly in the context of travel and show-business events.

Discussion topics in this community focus on TV shows, programs, videos, show business, sports, news, relationships, and pop stars (Dima Bilan). Propaganda terms are generally underpresent and appear mostly in the context of neutral news reports.

Community 1127: Sports Fans

Community 1127 is a medium-size community (8,056 members) within the more political metacommunity, organized around sports-related conversations. Prominent accounts are all dedicated to sports, including some that appear to be personal, with 60 to 70 tweets per day (@typographera and @stepanova_ka61). Overpresent terms are sports-related: *soccer, hockey, tennis, euro2016* (soccer championship), #KrivoiRog (Ukrainian city), and #Krivbass (basketball club). Politics and propaganda are underpresent, as are the terms *Russia, USA*, and *Ukraine*.

Community 1135: Ukrainian Business People

Community 1135 is a small community (147 users) within meta-community 2 that is interested in online commerce. Overpresent terms include Ukrainian geographic names (*Ukraine, Odessa*, and *Russia*) and Ukrainian news accounts (@replyua and @financeua). Other overpresent terms are related to commerce, including #aukro (online marketplace), *seller, price, buy, condition, hryvna, dollar*, and *production*. The discussion themes in this community are focused on business, finances, and sales. Poroshenko is often mentioned in a neutral context, as part of official news (signed a law or held a meeting), while Putin and Russia are often presented in a negative or sarcastic manner.

Community 1220: Russian Pop Music Fans

Community 1220 in metacommunity 2 is a medium-size community (7,480 members) centered on Russian pop singers. Overpresent accounts include those of popular Russian singers, such as @fkirkorov, @dkoldun, @nikolaibaskov, and @bilanofficial. Geographic terms that are overpresent include locations in Crimea, Russia, and Ukraine. Some other overpresent terms relate to filming, fashion, style, cars, and jewelry, and some commerce is also present with such terms as *personal ad*, *order*, and *hryvnas*. Propaganda is underpresent, and both Putin and Poroshenko are mentioned in a mostly neutral context.

Community 2435: Ukrainian News

Community 2435 is a small community (212 users) that is part of metacommunity 2 and is focused on sharing Ukrainian news. Overpresent users include pro-Ukraine news accounts @newsdaily_ukr and @novodvorskialex. Overpresent geographic names are Ukrainian: *Ukraine*, *Kyiv*, and *Zaporizhzhya*. Political terms are also specific to Ukraine: *Poroshenko*, *Savchenko* (Nadiya Savchenko, People's Deputy of Ukraine), *Lutsenko* (Yuriy Lutsenko, prosecutor general of Ukraine), *NABU* (National Anticorruption Bureau of Ukraine), and *Hryvnia* (the national currency of Ukraine).

Discussion themes focus on the news in Ukraine, with a lot of attention paid to the conflict in eastern Ukraine. Accounts use terms conventional for Ukrainian media and government officials. For example, the names of the republics *"LNR"* (Luganskaya Narodnaya Respublika, or Luhansk People's Republic) and *"DNR"* are used (with the quotation marks) and the term *guerillas* is used for separatists.

Putin, Russia, Novorossiya, and *DNR* are often mentioned in negative or sarcastic contexts.

Community 2613: Network of Bots

Community 2613, part of the more political metacommunity, appears to be a network of 1,108 bot accounts, consisting exclusively of accounts that follow and retweet each other. The majority of tweets from accounts in this community mention multiple other accounts for no reason and, with high regularity, post jokes, comments, and non-personal pictures from the internet. Many of the accounts post comments that make little or no sense but look like random computer-generated phrases. Although the majority of the content is generic pictures and jokes, there are occasionally pro-Russia, anti-Ukraine, and anti-U.S. hate posts.

From the overpresent terms in this community (#assessment [of property value], #realestate, #expertise, #apartment, #carassessment) and single consistent topic (real estate services in or near Kyiv), we believe that some company used this network to advertise real estate services to Twitter users during the period in which we gathered our data (May to July 2016).

Narrative Analysis of Pro-Ukraine and Pro-Russia Activist Communities

The Pro-Russia Activist Community (Community 4369)

When analyzing this community's tweet content, we found that the most overpresent terms are the accounts of Russian media outlets @zvezdanews, @rt_russian, and @lifenews_ru, as well as accounts of pseudonews websites devoted to propaganda: @rusnextru, @dnr_news, and @harkovnews. Pseudonews websites support the same pro-Kremlin narratives that regular Russian media promote, but often use more-radical expressions. Tweets from these accounts usually contain links to their respective websites.

Accounts that look private (not media outlets), such as @zapvv and @spacelordrock, are also popular within this community. Tweets from such accounts are mostly opinions about or interpretations of the current events, often accompanied by graphical images, but, as a rule, without reference to a source. The large number of tweets, more than 100,000 in the case of @zapvv, suggests that these accounts might be run by professional trolls.

The most overpresent terms, other than account names, include #RussianSpring, #Russia, *USA*, *VSU* (Ukrainian Armed Forces), #Novorossia, #news, *DNR*, #Belarus, and #DNR.

The aforementioned news and pseudonews accounts have the most influence: Retweets from them dominate the discussion in the community. Table B.1 shows that four out of the top five most overpresent word pairs are "rt" followed by the media account name.

Regarding the content of the narratives, propaganda presents Ukraine as a nationalist and fascist state, the United States as Russia's global competitor, and Russia as a place of progress and traditional values, confronting the decaying West. These narratives are supported by facts and stories that emphasize Crimea's historical belonging to

Table B.1
Top Ten Most Overpresent Word Pairs

Word Pair	Translation
rt @zvezdanews	
rt @rusnextru	
русская весна	Russian spring
rt @dnr_news	
rt @harkovnews	
телеканал «звезда»	Zvezda TV Channel
в киеве	In Kyiv
@zvezdanews в	@zvezdanews in
в россии	In Russia
в крыму	In Crimea

Russia, deny Russia's involvement in eastern Ukraine's conflict, blame the United States for interference in other countries' affairs, and praise Russia's military might.

Individual tweets from this community that had the highest number of retweets include the following:

- "This is agent Svyatogorov, chief of Bandera's assassination operation. Retweet if you believe he should be awarded a Hero Star posthumously" (praising those who killed Ukrainian nationalists)
- "If you write bad about Jews—anti-Semite; about blacks—racist; about gays—homophobe; about Russians—honest, brave, liberal journalist"
- "Yavlinskiy: Crimea should be returned to Ukraine. Yes? No? Retweet if you think Yavlinskiy should be returned to Ukraine" (bullying Russian opposition politician)
- "Picture: '300 Cossacks who did not surrender to fascists' was recognized as one of the best in the world" (picture showing Russia supporters, probably in Ukraine)
- "Russians: let's live in peace. USA General: Russians should be killed. Czech parliamentarian: Russians should be burned. Western media: Russians incite hatred[.]"

Examples of tweets from this community featuring some of the most overpresent keywords include the following:

- #RussianSpring
  - "Yenheniy Kiseliov: disgraceful journey from KGB agent to servant of Ukrainian nazis #RussianSpring http://rusnext.ru/news/1462979360" (referring to Russian journalist who moved to Kyiv)
  - "Racial war is starting in the US: Blacks demand imprisonment of policemen #RussianSpring http://rusnext.ru/news/1468141395"

- *Russia*
  - "Today Russia demonstrates to the public M-21 airplane, pride of national aviation building. Portfolio already includes dozens of orders"
  - "A bunch of vultures! G7 in Tokyo emphasized importance of dialogue with Russia and preserved all the sanctions"; a user named @SvetlanaForPutin replied, "We do not care! Russia only becomes stronger from their sanctions, those idiots suffer themselves."
- #Novorossia
  - "Ukrainian chasteners shelled 485 timed at DNR during the day #Novorossia"
  - "Awaiting large Ukrainian war http://goo.gl/fb/WaKBU7 #Novorossia" (the link to the article predicting start of a war)
  - "Poroshenko proposes to the West to do [ethnic] cleansing of DNR / LNR, following the example of Serbian Krajina http://od-novorossia.livejournal.com/1935579.html #Ukraine #Novorossia"
- *USA*
  - "USA started creeping intervention in Odessa. A thousand of American troops are marching in the city of Russian naval glory. Shame!!!"
  - "The most prominent Russophobes and critics of Russian government are on the USA payroll, everybody knows that"
  - "rt @zvezdanews American expert tells how USA supplies weapons to terrorists"
- *Crimea*
  - "You can steal from us Olympic Games—2016, World Cup—2018, but no one ever will steal Crimea—2014 from us #CrimeaIsOurs"
  - "I am ready to suffer any sanctions for Gergiev's concert in Palmira. For Olympic Sochi and happy Crimea, for returned National Pride!"
  - "The Washington Times: Russian S-400 will protect Crimea from NATO's 'air hooligans'"

- *Ukraine*
  - "John Perry, American journalist who exposed Irangate: satellite images related to MH17 show military personnel in Ukrainian uniforms next to the Buk missile system"
  - "On December 11 Poroshenko's Administration announced creation of cemetery for 250 thousand places. On March 5, 2015 Poroshenko signed an order to increase Ukrainian Army to 250 thousand. Ukrainians, when will you understand that Poroshenkos' nationalist regime under USA / EU guidance is simply destroying Ukraine's population?" (The text was posted as a picture, with an image of a burial ground and President Poroshenko.)
- *Kyiv*
  - "SBU launched surveillance of [OSCE, Organization for Security and Co-operation in Europe] observers to hide Kyiv's banned weapons"
  - "Kyiv's government are clowns of which we can only laugh"
  - "Russian expert: Instead of membership in NATO and EU Ukrainians will get status of plantation slaves"
- *VSU* (Ukrainian Armed Forces)
  - "@zvezdanews Tactics of decay: how Ukrainian Army destroys itself https://t.co/xtcstxlqeo #tvzvezad #donbas #vsu"
  - "@lifenews_ru Media: shelling by the vsu led to fire on Dokuchaevsk's factory. 38 mines over 20 minutes were launched on the city[.]"

The Pro-Ukraine Activist Community

The most-influential accounts in this community include @crimeaua1 and @krimrt, accounts devoted to Russian occupation of Crimea; @fake_midrf, an account exposing Russian actions, often in sarcastic form; and @inforesist, a news website account focusing on Russian aggression. The overpresent terms, which are not account names, include *rt*, #news, #Ukraine, #ua, #odessa, *Ukraine*, #Crimea, *RF* (Russian Federation), and #Donetsk.

Content of tweets covers a wide variety of topics and events, the majority of which can be linked to Ukraine or Russia. The common narrative is illegal Russian annexation of Crimea, occupation of Donbass, violation of human rights on those territories, and Ukraine's fight against Russia for territorial integrity. This narrative is supported by stories that expose Russian propaganda and support the actions of Ukraine and its partners.

Some of the most-retweeted posts from this community include the following:

- "Retweet if you believe these terrorist supporters should be prosecuted in Hague Tribunal" (picture of the two most prominent pro-Russia propagandists)
- "Nobody believe in Ukraine's victory, neither Europe nor US nor other countries. Retweet if you believe in our VICTORY! #Ukraine"
- "Screaming!" (sarcasm on propaganda blaming the United States for Russian internal problems: a video showing President Barack Obama destroying Russian transport infrastructure and taking benefits from Russian pensioners)
- "Special Forces from Kirovograd. Most of those on the photo have died defending our Motherland. Remember the Heroes!"
- "Why nobody loves them? Lithuania President refuses to answer questions from Russian journalists" (video of the moment)
- "Crimea will be returned to Ukraine in its original state: without electricity, water, or agriculture—as it was given to greedy Ukrainians in 1954 . . ."
- "Rada needs to adopt a law denying citizenship for separatism"
- "#Russia, you will never wash away the shame of a country-killer #War RT @euromaidan Night shelling from Russia[.]"

Pro-Russia Propaganda Lexical Analysis

In this appendix, we present the lexical analysis results for four different additional sources of Russian propaganda in order to quantitatively understand both the content and style of each and to understand the differences between what the Kremlin officially espouses and what others spread on Twitter.

Approach

We analyzed tweets from 84 different accounts from July 2015 to April 2016 as exemplars of different kinds of pro-Russia influencers. These data included 18 Twitter accounts of Russian officials (26,800 tweets), 39 Twitter accounts of pro-Russia news sources (239,000 tweets), 18 Twitter accounts from hand-confirmed pro-Russia trolls (668,000 tweets),[1] and nine Twitter accounts of thought leaders in Russian ideology (39,100 tweets).

The baseline corpus for this analysis was a data set consisting of 21.4 million Russian-language tweets from 227,000 users across Estonia, Latvia, Lithuania, Belarus, Ukraine, and Moldova. For each propaganda source, we performed keyness testing with log likelihood scoring to find the distinctive words in the source text, as compared with

---

[1] We identified troll accounts as suspicious if they had inhuman levels of volume and mentioned troll-favored hashtags, sites, or users. Once we identified a suspect account, we passed it to our Russian linguist, who personally inspected the accounts on Twitter. Sources used to inform this approach include Alexander, 2015a, and Shandra, 2016.

the baseline text (Baker et al., 2008; Scott, 2008, p. 110), akin to the first step of the resonance analysis procedure outlined in Appendix A. The list of keywords, together with their keyness scores, is referred to as a *signature*.

To verify that the computer-generated results were correct, we employed a human domain expert review of a sample of the keywords in each signature. We wanted the context-sensitive check of a human expert eye to ensure that those words made sense. If, for example, the signature consisted mostly of references to pop music, cooking, and fashion, the computer-based method likely did not accurately pull out the distinctive features of pro-Russia propaganda talk in the region. The rest of this section details the key features of each signature that our subject-matter expert considered informative.

Russian Officials

This data set consists of 26,800 tweets from 18 Twitter accounts of Kremlin officials, representative of Russia's political leadership. A large share of the keywords refer to political and policy issues, both domestic and international. The tone of tweets from which this signature comes is balanced and official, often positive, emphasizing hard efforts and successes of Russian government. For example, both *Medvedev* and #Medvedev are among the terms with the highest scores and are usually mentioned in a context of domestic politics (e.g., legislation on free economic zones, payments to families with children, financial transfers to local governments). *Zakharova* and *Lavrov*, representing the Russian MFA, are mentioned in a context of bilateral or multilateral international relations or MFA statements regarding events abroad. For example, one tweet states, "#Lavrov: The goal of Poroshenko's unclean statements is to break the 'genetic code' that unites our people." Terms related to military and conflict are often used in a context of Russia's defense minister's official statements on issues related to the armed forces and operation in Syria. Example tweets include "Shoigu: Pilot of Russian Airforce SU-24 was successfully rescued," "A workshop that installed explosives into cars near Aleppo was destroyed," and "Head of the General staff made a statement about downing of Russian SU-24 by Turkish Airforce."

Thirty-four percent of the keywords present in the official signature are unique terms not present in the other three signatures.[2] Unique terms with the highest keyness scores include #вво (Eastern Military District), #кпрф (Communist Party), #алеппо (Aleppo), *opposing* (as part of the name of the Russian Centre for Reconciliation of Opposing Sides in the Syrian Arab Republic), and *Neverov, Rashkin,* and *Zheleznyak* (all three are pro-Kremlin politicians).

Pro-Russia Thought Leaders

This data set consists of 39,100 tweets from nine Twitter accounts of thought leaders in Kremlin ideology. Tweets that form this signature are consistently promoting a pro-Russia view of the world, with a lot of focus abroad, emphasizing Russian roles and uniqueness. The signature has a high proportion of words related to conflict in Ukraine, portraying Ukraine negatively as an aggressor and the separatists as victims. Tweets examples include "Russia told UN [the United Nations] about shelling of hospitals in Donbass by Ukrainian troops," "Moscow warns about very high risk of escalation in Donbass," and "DNR Chief to America: keep your pet maniac leashed" (referring to Poroshenko). Western countries are often mentioned in the context of problems (both valid and false) facing the West, confrontation with Russia, and Russia's global supremacy, such as "British media ignored 150 thousand people marching in London," "British stop singing 'Rule, Britannia!' when a couple of TU-160 fly by. Coincidence? I do not think so!" "Korotchenko [Igor Korotchenko, a Russian journalist]: Navalniy [Alexei Navalniy, a politician and activist]—is an obedient tool of Western political will," "Syrian fighters are scared when they see how modern arms are used against ISIS," and "Russia beats USA in simplicity and price of arms. Russian arms have two advantages over American."

Twenty-two percent of the keywords in the thought leader signature are unique terms not present in the other three signatures. Unique terms with the highest scores include *Aramis* (name of the Russian propaganda movie about events in Donbass), *directive, Dugin (Dugin's*

---

[2] Note that we consider *word* and *#word* different terms.

Directive is a media program by the Russian radical nationalist Dugin), представьтесь (introduce yourself), and Бом (Michael Bohm, an American journalist and frequent guest of Russian political talk shows).

Media

This data set consisted of 239,000 tweets from 39 Twitter accounts of pro-Russia news sources. Tweets that form this signature are mostly news headlines, covering a wide variety of topics. The headlines are sometimes provocative, biased, or fake, and the largest share of terms can be classified as related to international issues. Both Ukrainian and Syrian conflicts are covered from Russia's perspective, often blaming Ukraine and the West for these conflicts. Examples include "Zhuravko [Aleksey Zhuravko, a writer]: 700 ISIS terrorists entered Kherson oblast, will start cutting heads soon," "NYT [*New York Times*]: NATO countries do not understand why Turkey shot down Russian SU-24," "Novorossiya—Syria: Donbass volunteers are ready to fight against ISIS," "Iran's MFA: USA actions in Syria crisis are very controversial," "Friendly neighbors: half of those refused entrance into Poland are Ukrainians," and "LNR is preparing for escalation of fighting from Ukraine."

Fifteen percent of the keywords in the media signature are unique terms not present in the other three signatures. Unique words include #риа, #tnt, *baltnews* (media companies), #mfa, *Donetsk*, *Riga* (in a context of news from Riga, Latvia), and *inomarka* (which means "foreign-made car" and is used in news reports that involve cars).

Trolls

The troll signature was formed using 668,000 tweets from 18 hand-confirmed Twitter accounts of pro-Kremlin trolls. The tweets that form this signature use less-formal language than those in the other signatures and are more likely to contain hate talk. Tweets are often anti-West, talking about threat and aggression in eastern Europe coming from NATO countries, Turkey's support of terrorists, and Russia's role in Syria. Terms inciting hatred or emphasizing supremacy, which are specific to more-radical propaganda, are ranked relatively high in this signature.[3]

About 17 percent of the keywords in the troll signature are unique terms that are not present in the other signatures. Some of the unique words with the highest keyness scores are offensive, such as майдаун, пиндос, укронацист, and хохлы (all are insulting words).

Signature Comparison

Each of the Russian propaganda signatures comes from a different source and contains subtle differences from the others. Some are official (such as the Russian political leaders), while others might or might not be state-directed (trolls and thought leaders). Table C.1 shows a small sample of translated keywords from each signature. Comparing the words used to describe the same topic or that fall into the same category (such as those that describe armed conflict) allows for a finer-grained understanding of the different language used by each propaganda source.

---

[3] Terms inciting hatred or emphasizing Russian supremacy are present in the other signatures but have lower keyness scores.

Table C.1
Select Keywords from Pro-Russia Propaganda Signatures

Category	Thought Leaders	Officials	Media	Trolls
Ukraine	Crimea, DNR, Donbass, Donetsk, LNR, Luhansk, Poroshenko, Ukrainian	agreement, crisis, dialogue, east, implementation	Avakov (the Ukrainian minister of the interior), Kharkov, DNR, Donbass, LNR, Ukrainian Armed Forces	armed forces, ATO (antiterrorist operation), Crimea, DNR, Gorlovka, LNR, names of various cities
Conflict	chastener, crime, dead, fighter, migrant, operation, refugee, shelling, terror, terrorist, victim	cease, crisis, fight, fighter, humanitarian, reconciliation	airstrike, attack, gang, refugee, shelling	attack, blockade, chaos, fighter, refugee, terrorism, war
International	Americans, British, Ministry of Foreign Affairs, OSCE, Syria, Turkey, UN, Washington, west	Aleppo, Egypt, embassy, Lavrov, Ministry of Foreign Affairs, representative, Syria, UN, Zakharova	Aleppo, American, anti-Russian, association, Austria, Azerbaijan, Belarus, ISIS, MFA, NATO, Syria, USA, visa-free	Assad, Belarus, geopolitics, ISIS, NATO, Poland, Syria, Turkey, USA, visa-free
Politics	member of parliament, minister, Navalniy (Russian opposition politician), opposition, political, Soviet Union, state	budget, Communist Party, education, government, legislation, Medvedev, member of parliament, minister, negotiations, parliament, people, state, voting	administration, Moscow, politics, Putin	administration, government, politics, president, USSR

Table C.1—Continued

Category	Thought Leaders	Officials	Media	Trolls
Military	*air and space forces, arms, military, Ministry of Defense, missile, nuclear, tank, threat*	*air and space forces, air force, armed, firing field, military, Ministry of Defense, positions, Shoygu* (Russian minister of defense), *unit*	*air base, air incident, artillery, base, battalion*	*air base, air strike, army, defense, nuclear, security*
Propaganda	n/a	n/a	n/a	*anti-fascist, bandera* (nationalist historical figure), *green men, polite men* (a term for combatants)
Prosaic	n/a	n/a	n/a	*absolutely, address, announce, nearest, poor*

NOTE: We derived these keywords from the top 100 words in each signature. Lexical and lexicogrammatical analyses work poorly at the level of individual utterances for just the reasons listed below—semantics and function at that level are highly context variable. However, at the level of aggregates, these methods have high validity and reliability because word and word-type aggregates that vary in statistically meaningful ways show structural differences in text collections. This often seems counterintuitive to people outside of corpus linguistics and natural language processing because we as human readers experience only *serial reading*: one sentence at a time, doing human-level fine-grained context work, but never able to see large-scale statistical patterns. Although we are combining this kind of aggregate-level lexical analysis with SNA in a novel fashion, decades of empirical work in corpus (that is, *aggregate*) linguistics support the reality that quantified lists of statistically variant words *do* have meaning.

Interview Protocol

This appendix reproduces, unedited, our interview protocol.

Consent

The RAND Corporation, a non-profit policy research institution, is seeking to understand how the United States and NATO can best counter Russian propaganda on social media. As part of this effort, we are conducting an analysis of Russian social media. This analysis is focused on understanding the nature and impact of Russian outreach on social media to Russia's neighboring states of Estonia, Latvia, Ukraine, Lithuania, Belarus and Moldova.

We would like to solicit your feedback on how the U.S., NATO, and Russia's neighboring states can best counter Russian propaganda on social media.

We anticipate that this interview will only take 30–60 minutes. We have identified five broad topics that can guide our conversation. Thank-you for your participation.

1. What threat does Russian propaganda on social media pose to Russia's neighboring states in Eastern Europe (Estonia, Latvia, Ukraine[,] Lithuania, Belarus and Moldova)?
   a. What is the nature of Russia's social media engagement with these countries?
   b. How does Russian social media threaten U.S. and Western European interests, if at all?

2. How do the U.S., NATO, EU or other relevant organizations currently work to counter Russian propaganda on social media?
   a. How do Russia's neighboring states work to counter this threat?
3. What are the key limitations or challenges with the U.S. and international response? What about the response of Russia's neighboring states?
   a. What about organization, training, legal, intelligence, resource, and or political constraints?
4. How can the U.S., its allies, partners, and relevant organizations improve their response?
   a. Please identify any critical DOTMLPF (Doctrine, Organization, Training, Manpower, Leadership & Education, Personnel, and Facilities) implications[.]
   b. What should be the role of particular services, departments and agencies in understanding or responding to Russian social media?
   c. Are there specific programs that the U.S. Department of Defense, State Department, or other government organizations should pursue to strengthen allied or partner capacity?
   d. What should be the respective role of government compared with NGOs, media organizations, or other private actors?
5. Who else should we speak to? What other questions must we ask?

This project is led by Todd Helmus and Elizabeth Bodine-Baron and it is being sponsored by the U.S. Government. For more information, please contact Todd at (703) 413-1100 x5231/helmus@rand.org or Elizabeth at (310) 393-0411 x7501/ebodineb@rand.org.

As with any important topic there might be risks if your specific comments were made known outside the research team. Risks associated with such a disclosure might increase if, for example, you provide comments that were critical of your agency or employer. However, RAND will keep the information you provide confidential and will not release it without your permission, except as required by law. We are following procedures to ensure that there will not be any inadvertent release of information including: Removing all direct identifiers such as your name and contact information from the interview notes; Storing all interview notes in a password protected computer; and Destroying all interview notes once the project is complete.

Attribution and Voluntary Participation

We will be preparing a report based on this and other interviews and we plan to include some quotes from our respondents. We will treat your remarks as confidential and will not cite you in connection with anything you say. Your participation in this interview is entirely voluntary—you should feel free to decline or you may choose not to answer any given question. Your decision will not affect your relationship with RAND. Do you have any questions? Do you agree to participate in this interview? [Mark response on interview form guide]

If you have any questions or concerns about your rights as a research subject, please contact the Human Subjects Protection Committee at (866) 697-5620 or hspcinfo@rand.org. The mailing address is Human Subjects Protection Committee, RAND, 1700 Main Street, Santa Monica, CA 90407.

References

"About Snopes.com," *Snopes*, undated; last accessed July 10, 2017. As of July 10, 2017:
http://www.snopes.com/about-snopes/

Alexander, Lawrence, "Social Network Analysis Reveals Full Scale of Kremlin's Twitter Bot Campaign," *Global Voices*, April 2, 2015a. As of January 3, 2016:
https://globalvoices.org/2015/04/02/analyzing-kremlin-twitter-bots/

———, "Do Russian Media Get a Boost from Bots on Twitter?" *Global Investigative Journalism Network*, December 3, 2015b. As of January 3, 2017:
http://gijn.org/2015/12/03/do-russian-media-get-a-boost-from-bots-on-twitter/#

"America's Answer to Russian Propaganda TV," *Economist*, June 15, 2017. As of November 4, 2017:
http://www.economist.com/news/united-states/21723449-current-time-broadcasts-russian-capitol-hill-americas-answer-russian-propaganda

Annenkov, Yuri, *Dnevnik moikh vstrech: tsikl tragedii* [People and portraits: A tragic cycle], New York: Inter-Language Literary Associates, 1966.

Aro, Jessikka, "The Cyberspace War: Propaganda and Trolling as Warfare Tools," *European View*, Vol. 15, No. 1, June 2016, pp. 121–132. As of January 3, 2017:
http://link.springer.com/article/10.1007/s12290-016-0395-5

Auers, Daunis, *Comparative Politics and Government of the Baltic States: Estonia, Latvia and Lithuania in the 21st Century*, New York: Palgrave Macmillan, 2015.

Baker, Paul, Costas Gabrielatos, Majid Khosravinik, Michał Krzyżanowski, Tony McEnery, and Ruth Wodak, "A Useful Methodological Synergy? Combining Critical Discourse Analysis and Corpus Linguistics to Examine Discourses of Refugees and Asylum Seekers in the UK Press," *Discourse and Society*, Vol. 19, No. 3, 2008, pp. 273–306.

BBG—*See* Broadcasting Board of Governors.

"Besporyadki pod Radoy gotovili grazhdane RF v sotsseti «VKontakte»—SBU" [Riots under the Rada were organized by Russian citizens through VKontakte—Security Service], Independent News Bureau, October 15, 2014. As of November 8, 2017:
http://nbnews.com.ua/ru/news/134239/

"Beware of NGOs, They Are Evil," *Disinformation Review*, Issue 51, December 13, 2016. As of February 3, 2017:
http://us11.campaign-archive2.com/
?u=cd23226ada1699a77000eb60b&id=e8ff4a887e&e=9edf89f27f

Bodine-Baron, Elizabeth, Todd Helmus, Madeline Magnuson, and Zev Winkelman, *Examining ISIS Support and Opposition Networks on Twitter*, Santa Monica, Calif.: RAND Corporation, RR-1328-RC, 2016. As of December 18, 2017:
https://www.rand.org/pubs/research_reports/RR1328.html

Boffey, Daniel, "Europe's New Cold War Turns Digital as Vladimir Putin Expands Media Offensive," *Guardian*, March 5, 2016. As of January 3, 2016:
https://www.theguardian.com/world/2016/mar/05/
europe-vladimir-putin-russia-social-media-trolls

Borogan, Irina, journalist, and Andrei Soldatov, journalist, "Diplomacy, Economics, and Force in the Emerging International Order," briefing given to the authors, September 13, 2016.

Borthwick, John, "Media Hacking," *Render-from-betaworks*, March 7, 2015. As of January 3, 2017:
https://medium.com/render-from-betaworks/media-hacking-3b1e350d619c#.mmowrfvh8

Botometer, home page, undated. As of November 8, 2017:
https://botometer.iuni.iu.edu/#!/

Broadcasting Board of Governors, "BBG Launches 24/7 Russian-Language Network," *PR Newswire*, February 7, 2017.

Center for Media Literacy, "About CML," undated. As of July 10, 2017:
http://www.medialit.org/about-cml

Chen, Adrian, "The Agency," *New York Times*, June 2, 2015. As of January 3, 2017:
http://www.nytimes.com/2015/06/07/magazine/the-agency.html

Clauset, Aaron, M. E. J. Newman, and Cristopher Moore, "Finding Community Structure in Very Large Networks," *Physical Review E*, Vol. 70, No. 6, December 2004.

Confessore, Nicholas, and Daisuke Wakabayashi, "How Russia Harvested American Rage to Reshape U.S. Politics," *New York Times*, October 9, 2017. As of October 15, 2018:
https://www.nytimes.com/2017/10/09/technology/
russia-election-facebook-ads-rage.html

"Daily Chart: Propaganda and Social Media," *Economist*, September 8, 2016. As of January 3, 2017:
http://www.economist.com/blogs/graphicdetail/2016/09/daily-chart-4

Digital Forensic Research Lab, Atlantic Council, "Electronic Warfare by Drone and SMS: How Russia-Backed Separatists Use 'Pinpoint Propaganda' in the Donbas," *Medium.com*, May 18, 2017. As of July 10, 2017:
https://medium.com/dfrlab/electronic-warfare-by-drone-and-sms-7fec6aa7d696

"Disinformation Review Issue 51," December 13, 2016. As of January 16, 2017:
https://eeas.europa.eu/sites/eeas/files/disinformation_review_13.12.2016_eng.pdf

"Disinformation Review Issue 52," December 20, 2016. As of January 16, 2017:
https://eeas.europa.eu/sites/eeas/files/disinformation_review_20.12.2016_eng.pdf

"Disinformation Review Issue 53," January 12, 2017. As of January 16, 2017:
https://eeas.europa.eu/sites/eeas/files/disinformation_review_12.01.2017_eng.pdf

Duncan, Jessica, "Russia Launches a 'Troll Factory' Using Fake Twitter and Facebook Accounts to Flood Social Media with Lies About Britain and the West," *Daily Mail*, October 16, 2016. As of January 3, 2017:
http://www.dailymail.co.uk/news/article-3840816/Russia-launches-troll-factory-using-fake-Twitter-Facebook-accounts-flood-social-media-lies-Britain-West.html

"Fake: Merkel for Ending Russian Sanctions," *StopFake*, May 4, 2017. As of July 10, 2017:
http://www.stopfake.org/en/fake-merkel-for-ending-russia-sanctions/

"Fake: Ukraine's Falling Credit Rating," *StopFake*, May 3, 2017. As of November 9, 2017:
https://www.stopfake.org/en/fake-ukraine-s-falling-credit-rating/

Freedom House, "Freedom of the Press 2015: Latvia," c. 2015. As of July 10, 2017:
https://freedomhouse.org/report/freedom-press/2015/latvia

————, "Freedom on the Net 2016: Russia," c. 2016. As of November 4, 2017:
https://freedomhouse.org/report/freedom-net/2016/russia

Frenett, Ross, founder, MoonshotCVE, Washington, D.C., interview with the authors, June 26, 2017.

GemiusAudience, "Internet-auditoriya Uaneta za mart 2015 goda," May 6, 2015. As of November 8, 2017:
https://www.slideshare.net/LesyaPrus/2015-47812786

General Secretariat of the Council, European Council, "European Council Meeting (19 and 20 March 2015): Conclusions," EUCO 11/15, March 20, 2015. As of July 10, 2017:
http://data.consilium.europa.eu/doc/document/ST-11-2015-INIT/en/pdf

Gerber, Theodore P., and Jane Zavisca, "Does Russian Propaganda Work?" *Washington Quarterly*, Summer 2016, pp. 79–98.

Giles, Keir, "Russia's 'New' Tools for Confronting the West: Continuity and Innovation in Moscow's Exercise of Power," Chatham House, Russia and Eurasia Programme, March 21, 2016. As of January 3, 2017:
https://www.chathamhouse.org/sites/files/chathamhouse/publications/research/2016-03-21-russias-new-tools-giles.pdf

GNIP, "Profile Geo 2.0," undated. As of November 8, 2017:
http://support.gnip.com/enrichments/profile_geo.html

Goldsberry, Joshua, Dawn Goldsberry, and Paras Sharma, Alqimi National Security, "Russian Trollololing," presentation, December 2015.

Greenberg, Andy, "Now Anyone Can Deploy Google's Troll-Fighting AI," *Wired*, February 23, 2017. As of July 10, 2017:
https://www.wired.com/2017/02/googles-troll-fighting-ai-now-belongs-world/

Hanneman, Robert A., and Mark Riddle, *Introduction to Social Network Methods*, Riverside, Calif.: University of California, 2005.

Hauser, Gerard A., *Introduction to Rhetorical Theory*, Prospect Heights, Ill.: Waveland Press, 2002.

Helmus, Todd, and Elizabeth Bodine-Baron, *Empowering ISIS Opponents on Twitter*, Santa Monica, Calif.: RAND Corporation, PE-227-RC, 2017. As of November 5, 2017:
https://www.rand.org/pubs/perspectives/PE227.html

InMind, *Media Consumption Survey: Ukraine 2016*, U.S. Agency for International Development, U-Media Project, August 2016.

International Broadcasting Multimedia Platform of Ukraine, home page, undated. As of November 9, 2017:
http://www.uatv.pro/

"Internet Usage in Latvia," *AdCombo Blog*, February 2, 2017. As of November 8, 2017:
https://adcombo-blog.com/internet-usage-latvia/

Jolls, Tessa, director, Center for Media Literacy, telephone interview with the authors, July 7, 2017.

Kasekamp, Andres, *A History of the Baltic States*, New York: Palgrave Macmillan, 2010.

Kaufer, David S., and Brian S. Butler, *Rhetoric and the Arts of Design*, Mahwah, N.J.: L. Erlbaum Associates, 2010.

Khmelko, V. E., *Linhvo-etnichna struktura Ukrayiny: Rehional'ni osoblyvosti ta tendentsiyi zmin za roky nezalezhnosti* [Ethno-linguistic structure of Ukraine: Regional features and tendencies of changes during independence], undated. As of November 4, 2017:
http://www.kiis.com.ua/materials/articles_HVE/16_linguaethnical.pdf

Kivirähk, Juhan, "Integrating Estonia's Russian-Speaking Population: Findings of National Defense Opinion Surveys," International Centre for Defence and Security, December 31, 2014. As of November 5, 2017:
https://www.icds.ee/publications/article/integrating-estonias-russian-speaking-population-findings-of-national-defense-opinion-surveys/

Kogan, Rami, "Bedep Trojan Malware Spread by the Angler Exploit Kit Gets Political," *SpiderLabs Blog*, April 29, 2015. As of February 10, 2017:
https://www.trustwave.com/Resources/SpiderLabs-Blog/
Bedep-trojan-malware-spread-by-the-Angler-exploit-kit-gets-political/

Kokotyukh, Andriy, *Chomu ukrayins'ki telekanaly ne pospishayut' ozbroyuvatysya ukrayins'kymy serialamy* [Why Ukrainian TV channels are not rushing to buy Ukrainian TV shows], *Espreso.tv*, March 25, 2015. As of July 10, 2017:
http://ua.espreso.tv/article/2015/03/25/chomu_ukrayinski_telekanaly_ne_
pospishayut_ozbroyuvatysya_ukrayinskymy_serialamy

Konsolidatsiya Ukrayins'koho suspil'stva: Shlyakhy, vyklyky, perspektyvy—Informatsiyno-analitychni materialy do fakhovoyi dyskusiyi, 16 hrudnya 2016r [Consolidation of Ukrainian society: Ways, challenges, perspectives—Information and analytical materials to the professional discussion, December 16, 2016], c. 2016. As of November 9, 2017:
http://old.razumkov.org.ua/upload/Identi-2016.pdf

Laitin, David D., *Identity in Formation: The Russian-Speaking Populations in the New Abroad*, Ithaca, N.Y.: Cornell University Press, 1998.

"Latvia's Foreign Minister Asks US Embassy to Quit Using Russian Language," *Sputnik*, August 28, 2016. As of November 4, 2017:
https://sputniknews.com/europe/201608281044705599-us-embassy-uses-russian/

Lough, John, Orysia Lutsevych, Peter Pomerantsev, Stanislav Secrieru, and Anton Shekhovtsov, "Russian Influence Abroad: Non-State Actors and Propaganda," Chatham House, Russia and Eurasia Programme Meeting Summary, October 24, 2014. As of January 3, 2017:
https://www.chathamhouse.org/sites/files/chathamhouse/field/field_document/
20141024RussianInfluenceAbroad.pdf

Lucas, Edward, "Russia Turned Me into Propaganda," *Daily Beast*, August 20, 2015. As of January 16, 2017:
http://www.thedailybeast.com/articles/2015/08/20/
russia-turned-me-into-propaganda.html

Luhn, Alec, "Ex-Soviet Countries on Front Line of Russia's Media War with the West," *Guardian*, January 6, 2015. As of January 3, 2016:
https://www.theguardian.com/world/2015/
jan/06/-sp-ex-soviet-countries-front-line-russia-media-propaganda-war-west

MacFarquhar, Neil, "A Powerful Russian Weapon: The Spread of False Stories," *New York Times*, August 28, 2016. As of January 3, 2017:
http://www.nytimes.com/2016/08/29/world/europe/russia-sweden-disinformation.
html

McCarthy, Tom, "How Russia Used Social Media to Divide Americans," *Guardian*, October 14, 2017. As of October 15, 2017:
https://www.theguardian.com/us-news/2017/oct/14/
russia-us-politics-social-media-facebook

Miller, Christopher, "Ukraine Just Created Its Own Version of Orwell's 'Ministry of Truth,'" *Mashable*, December 2, 2014. As of July 10, 2017:
http://mashable.com/2014/12/02/ukraine-ministry-of-truth/#FvTtcWJFsOqG

Miniwatts Marketing Group, "Internet in Europe Stats," *Internet World Stats*, updated November 3, 2017. As of November 8, 2017:
http://www.internetworldstats.com/stats4.htm

Moore, Alfred, "Talking Politics Online: Why Everything Should Be Connected," *Challenges to Democracy*, September 7, 2016. As of July 10, 2017:
http://www.challengestodemocracy.us/home/
talking-politics-online-why-not-everything-should-be-connected/#sthash.
GGzjhZZ9.dpbs

Moore, Charles, brigadier general, deputy director of the Joint Staff for global operations, "Testimony Before the House Subcommittee on Emerging Threats and Capabilities: Witness Statement of Brig Gen Charles Moore, Deputy Director for Global Operations, Joint Staff," October 22, 2015. As of July 10, 2017:
http://docs.house.gov/meetings/AS/AS26/20151022/104086/
HHRG-114-AS26-Wstate-MooreUSAFC-20151022.pdf

"Mystery Website Producer Has Ties to Harmony, LTV Reports," *LSM.lv*, January 9, year unknown. As of November 9, 2017:
http://eng.lsm.lv/article/society/defense/
mystery-website-producer-has-ties-to-harmony-ltv-reports.a218258/

Nekrasov, Vsevolod, "Ukrayins'kyy analoh 'Russia Today': Inozemne movlennya chy kursy dlya perukariv?" [Ukrainian analogue of 'Russia Today': International broadcasting or hairdressing courses?], *Ukrainska Pravda*, August 29, 2016. As of July 10, 2017:
http://www.epravda.com.ua/publications/2016/08/29/603329/

Nimmo, Ben, "Lisa 2.0: How Pro-Kremlin Media in Germany Have Been Using a New Fake to Justify an Old One," *StopFake*, March 14, 2017. As of September 27, 2017:
http://www.stopfake.org/en/lisa-2-0-how-pro-kremlin-media-in-germany-have-been-using-a-new-fake-to-justify-an-old-one/

Office of the Director of National Intelligence, National Intelligence Council, *Assessing Russian Activities and Intentions in Recent US Elections*, Intelligence Community Assessment 2017-01D, January 6, 2017. As of February 10, 2017:
https://www.dni.gov/files/documents/ICA_2017_01.pdf

Office of the Under Secretary of Defense (Comptroller), *European Reassurance Initiative: Department of Defense Budget Fiscal Year (FY) 2017*, February 2016. As of July 10, 2017:
http://comptroller.defense.gov/Portals/45/Documents/defbudget/fy2017/FY2017_ERI_J-Book.pdf

"Plan for Suppression of Eastern Ukraine Prepared by US Agency RAND for Poroshenko," *Voice of Russia*, July 5, 2014. As of January 18, 2017:
https://sputniknews.com/voiceofrussia/news/2014_07_05/Plan-for-suppression-of-eastern-Ukraine-prepared-by-US-Agency-RAND-for-Poroshenko-2636/

Pomerantsev, Peter, and Michael Weiss, *The Menace of Unreality: How the Kremlin Weaponizes Information, Culture and Money: A Special Report Presented by the Interpreter, a Project of the Institute of Modern Russia*, Institute of Modern Russia, 2014. As of November 5, 2017:
https://imrussia.org/media/pdf/Research/Michael_Weiss_and_Peter_Pomerantsev__The_Menace_of_Unreality.pdf

Priest, Dana, and Michael Birnbaum, "Europe Has Been Working to Expose Russian Meddling for Years," *Washington Post*, June 25, 2017. As of July 10, 2017:
https://www.washingtonpost.com/world/europe/europe-has-been-working-to-expose-russian-meddling-for-years/2017/06/25/e42dcece-4a09-11e7-9669-250d0b15f83b_story.html?utm_term=.72df4f865bb2

PropOrNot Team, "Black Friday Report: On Russian Propaganda Network Mapping," November 26, 2016. As of January 3, 2017:
https://drive.google.com/file/d/0Byj_1ybuSGp_NmYtRF95VTJTeUk/view

Public Law 107-56, Uniting and Strengthening America by Providing Appropriate Tools Required to Intercept and Obstruct Terrorism Act of 2001, October 26, 2001. As of November 8, 2017:
https://www.gpo.gov/fdsys/pkg/PLAW-107publ56

Public Law 114-328, National Defense Authorization Act for Fiscal Year 2017, December 23, 2016. As of November 9, 2017:
https://www.gpo.gov/fdsys/pkg/PLAW-114publ328/content-detail.html

Radin, Andrew, *Hybrid Warfare in the Baltics: Threats and Potential Responses*, Santa Monica, Calif.: RAND Corporation, RR-1577-AF, 2017. As of November 5, 2017:
https://www.rand.org/pubs/research_reports/RR1577.html

Radin, Andrew, and Clinton Bruce Reach, *Russian Views of the International Order*, Santa Monica, Calif.: RAND Corporation, RR-1826-OSD, 2017. As of January 27, 2018:
https://www.rand.org/pubs/research_reports/RR1826.html

Rapawy, Stephen, *Ethnic Reidentification in Ukraine*, Washington, D.C.: U.S. Bureau of the Census, Population Division, International Programs Center Staff Paper 90, August 1997.

Redirect Method, home page, undated. As of November 5, 2017:
https://redirectmethod.org/

Romaniuk, Anatole, and Oleksandr Gladun, "Demographic Trends in Ukraine: Past, Present, and Future," *Population and Development Review*, Vol. 41, No. 2, June 2015, pp. 315–337.

Safire, William, "On Language," *New York Times*, April 12, 1987. As of October 20, 2017:
http://www.nytimes.com/1987/04/12/magazine/on-language.html

Samokhvalova, Lana, "The Russian Organizers of a 'Third Maidan' in Ukraine," *Euromaidan Press*, February 14, 2016. As of July 10, 2017:
http://euromaidanpress.com/2016/02/14/
the-russian-organizers-of-a-third-maidan-in-ukraine/#arvlbdata

"SBU porushyla kryminal'nu spravu za rozpovsyudzhennya motoroshnykh chutok pro Ukrayins'kykh viys'kovykh" [The SBU dismissed the criminal disclaimer for the distribution of motorships in Ukrainian military missions], *TSN*, January 6, 2015. As of July 10, 2017:
https://tsn.ua/politika/sbu-porushila-kriminalnu-spravu-za-rozpovsyudzhennya-motoroshnih-chutok-pro-ukrayinskih-viyskovih-401207.html

Scott, M., "Mapping Key Words to Problem and Solution," in Mike Scott and Geoff Thompson, eds., *Patterns of Text: In Honour of Michael Hoey*, Amsterdam: Benjamins, 2008, pp. 109–127.

Shandra, Alya, "Twitter's New Policy Misused by Pro-Kremlin Accounts to Block Ukrainian Bloggers #SaveUaTwi," *Euromaidan Press*, January 9, 2016. As of November 7, 2017:
http://euromaidanpress.com/2016/01/09/twitters-new-policy-misused-by-pro-kremlin-accounts-to-attack-top-ukrainian-bloggers-saveuatwi/

Sharkov, Damien, "35,000 Volunteers Sign Up for Ukraine's 'Information Army' on First Day," *Newsweek*, February 27, 2015. As of December 18, 2017:
http://www.newsweek.com/
35000-volunteers-sign-ukraines-information-army-first-day-310121

"Shtab ATO: Chutky pro vidstup ZSU—Informatsiyna provokatsiya Rosiys'kykh okupantiv" [ATO headquarters: Rumors about Ukrainian Army retreat are Russian informational provocation], *5.ua*, May 30, 2014. As of July 10, 2017:
https://www.5.ua/suspilstvo/shtab-ato-chutky-pro-vidstup-zsu-informatsiina-provokatsiia-rosiiskykh-okupantiv-115591.html

Shulman, Stephen, "The Contours of Civic and Ethnic National Identification in Ukraine," *Europe–Asia Studies*, Vol. 56, No. 1, January 2004, pp. 35–56.

Smith, Oli, "Russia's Fake Ukraine War Report Exposed in Putin PR Disaster," *Express*, August 24, 2015. As of January 16, 2017:
http://www.express.co.uk/news/world/600413/
Russia-s-fake-Ukraine-war-report-exposed-Putin-PR-disaster

Smyth, Regina, and Sarah Oates, "Mind the Gaps: Media Use and Mass Action in Russia," *Europe–Asia Studies*, Vol. 67, No. 2, March 2015, pp. 285–305.

Snyder, Timothy, "Ukrainian Extremists Will Only Triumph If Russia Invades," *New Republic*, April 17, 2014. As of November 4, 2017:
https://newrepublic.com/article/117395/
historic-ukrainian-russian-relations-impact-maidan-revolution

Sulleyman, Aatif, "Here Is Facebook's Guide to Fake News," *Independent*, May 9, 2017. As of July 10, 2017:
http://www.independent.co.uk/news/facebook-fake-news-guide-articles-curate-stop-take-down-lies-russia-donald-trump-us-politics-a7726111.html

Szwed, Robert, *Framing of the Ukraine–Russia Conflict in Online and Social Media*, Riga, Latvia: North Atlantic Treaty Organization Strategic Communications Centre of Excellence, May 2016. As of January 19, 2016:
http://www.stratcomcoe.org/
framing-ukraine-russia-conflict-online-and-social-media

"The Times Is Partnering with Jigsaw to Expand Comment Capabilities," *New York Times*, September 20, 2016. As of July 10, 2017:
http://www.nytco.com/
the-times-is-partnering-with-jigsaw-to-expand-comment-capabilities/

Thomas, Timothy, "Russia's 21st Century Information War: Working to Undermine and Destabilize Populations," *Defence Strategic Communications*, Vol. 1, No. 1, Winter 2015, pp. 11–26. As of November 7, 2017:
https://www.stratcomcoe.org/timothy-thomas-russias-21st-century-information-war-working-undermine-and-destabilize-populations

Timberg, Craig, "Russian Propaganda Effort Helped Spread 'Fake News' During Election, Experts Say," *Washington Post*, November 24, 2016. As of January 3, 2016:
https://www.washingtonpost.com/business/economy/
russian-propaganda-effort-helped-spread-fake-news-during-election-experts-say/
2016/11/24/793903b6-8a40-4ca9-b712-716af66098fe_story.
html?utm_term=.82ee94754e1d

Twitter, "About Verified Accounts," undated. As of July 10, 2017:
https://support.twitter.com/articles/119135#

UA|TV—*See* International Broadcasting Multimedia Platform of Ukraine.

"Ukraine Bans Its Top Social Networks Because They Are Russian," *Economist*, May 19, 2017. As of November 9, 2017:
https://www.economist.com/news/europe/21722360-blocking-websites-may-be-pointless-it-could-help-president-poroshenkos-popularity-ukraine

"V Ukrayini vzhe zaboronyly 73 rosiys'ki telekanaly" [73 Russian TV channels are already banned in Ukraine], *ZN,ua*, September 7, 2016. As of November 4, 2017:
https://dt.ua/UKRAINE/
v-ukrayini-vzhe-zaboronili-73-rosiyski-telekanali-218142_.html

Vatsov, Dimitar, and Milena Iakimova, "Co-Opting Discontent: Russian Propaganda in the Bulgarian Media," *StopFake*, October 27, 2017. As of January 2, 2018:
https://www.stopfake.org/en/
co-opting-discontent-russian-propaganda-in-the-bulgarian-media/

Walker, Shaun, "Salutin' Putin: Inside a Russian Troll House," *Guardian*, April 2, 2015. As of February 10, 2017:
http://www.theguardian.com/world/2015/apr/02/
putin-kremlin-inside-russian-troll-house

Weisburd, Andrew, Clint Watts, and J. M. Berger, "Trolling for Trump: How Russia Is Trying to Destroy Our Democracy," *War on the Rocks*, November 6, 2016. As of November 8, 2017:
https://warontherocks.com/2016/11/
trolling-for-trump-how-russia-is-trying-to-destroy-our-democracy/

Wilson, Andrew, "Four Types of Russian Propaganda," *Aspen Review*, Issue 4, 2015. As of November 7, 2017:
https://www.aspenreview.com/article/2017/four-types-of-russian-propaganda/

Zakem, Vera, Paul Saunders, and Daniel Antoun, *Mobilizing Compatriots: Russia's Strategy, Tactics, and Influence in the Former Soviet Union*, CNA, November 2015. As of January 3, 2017:
https://www.cna.org/CNA_files/PDF/DOP-2015-U-011689-1Rev.pdf